THE HOLOCAUST
THE BASICS

The Holocaust: The Basics is a concise introduction to the study of this seismic event in mid twentieth-century human history.

The book takes an original approach as both a narrative and thematic introduction to the topic, and provides a core foundation for readers embarking upon their own study. It examines a range of perspectives and subjects surrounding the Holocaust, including:

- the perpetrators of the Holocaust
- the victims
- resistance to the Holocaust
- liberation
- legacies and survivors' memories of the Holocaust.

Supported by a chronology, glossary, questions for discussion, and boxed case studies that focus the reader's thoughts and develop their appreciation of the subjects considered more broadly, *The Holocaust: The Basics* is the ideal introduction to this controversial and widely debated topic for both students and the more general reader.

Paul R. Bartrop is Professor of History and Director of the Center for Judaic, Holocaust, and Genocide Studies at Florida Gulf Coast University, Fort Myers, USA. He is the author or editor of over twenty books, including the Routledge titles *Genocide: The Basics* (2015); *Fifty Key Thinkers on the Holocaust and Genocide* (2011); and *The Genocide Studies Reader* (2009).

THE BASICS SERIES

NARRATIVE
BRONWEN THOMAS

PHILOSOPHY (FIFTH EDITION)
NIGEL WARBURTON

POETRY (THIRD EDITION)
JEFFREY WAINWRIGHT

THE QUR'AN (SECOND EDITION)
MASSIMO CAMPANINI

RACE AND ETHNICITY
PETER KIVISTO AND PAUL R. CROLL

RELIGION (SECOND EDITION)
MALORY NYE

RELIGION AND SCIENCE
PHILIP CLAYTON

RESEARCH METHODS (SECOND EDITION)
NICHOLAS WALLIMAN

ROMAN CATHOLICISM (SECOND EDITION)
MICHAEL WALSH

SHAKESPEARE (THIRD EDITION)
SEAN MCEVOY

TERRORISM
JAMES LUTZ AND BRENDA LUTZ

WITCHCRAFT
MARION GIBSON

WOMEN'S STUDIES
BONNIE SMITH

WORLD HISTORY
PETER N. STEARNS

RESEARCH METHODS
NICHOLAS WALLIMAN

THE HOLOCAUST
PAUL R. BARTROP

For a full list of titles in this series, please visit www.routledge.com/The-Basics/book-series/B

THE HOLOCAUST
THE BASICS

Paul R. Bartrop

LONDON AND NEW YORK

First published 2020
by Routledge
2 Park Square, Milton Park, Abingdon, Oxon OX14 4RN

and by Routledge
52 Vanderbilt Avenue, New York, NY 10017

Routledge is an imprint of the Taylor & Francis Group, an informa business

© 2020 Paul R. Bartrop

The right of Paul R. Bartrop to be identified as author of this work has been asserted by him in accordance with sections 77 and 78 of the Copyright, Designs and Patents Act 1988.

All rights reserved. No part of this book may be reprinted or reproduced or utilised in any form or by any electronic, mechanical, or other means, now known or hereafter invented, including photocopying and recording, or in any information storage or retrieval system, without permission in writing from the publishers.

Trademark notice: Product or corporate names may be trademarks or registered trademarks, and are used only for identification and explanation without intent to infringe.

British Library Cataloguing-in-Publication Data
A catalogue record for this book is available from the British Library

Library of Congress Cataloging-in-Publication Data
Names: Bartrop, Paul R. (Paul Robert), 1955- author.
Title: The Holocaust : the basics / Paul R. Bartrop.
Description: First edition. | New York : Taylor and Francis, [2019] |
Includes bibliographical references and index. |
Identifiers: LCCN 2019010298 (print) | LCCN 2019010672 (ebook)
Subjects: LCSH: Holocaust, Jewish (1939-1945)--History.
Classification: LCC D804.3 (ebook) | LCC D804.3 .B36365 2019 (print) |
DDC 940.53/18--dc23
LC record available at https://lccn.loc.gov/2019010298

ISBN: 978-1-138-57418-2 (hbk)
ISBN: 978-1-138-57419-9 (pbk)
ISBN: 978-0-203-70119-5 (ebk)

Typeset in Bembo
by Swales & Willis, Exeter, Devon, UK

CONTENTS

	List of Boxes	vi
	Preface	vii
1	Introduction: Defining the Holocaust	1
2	Outlines, Origins, and Consequences	8
3	Perpetrators of the Holocaust	23
4	Jews and Other Victims	49
5	Rescue from the Third Reich and the Holocaust	66
6	Resistance during the Holocaust	96
7	Ending the Holocaust	117
8	Survivors Reflect on the Holocaust	131
9	Conclusion: Holocaust Memory and the Future	145
	Glossary	159
	Chronology	167
	Bibliography	177
	Index	189

BOXES

2.1	A Child's Experience: Shirley Berger Gottesman	12
3.1	Portrait of a Perpetrator: Rudolf Hoess	31
4.1	Portrait of a Survivor: Fred Spiegel	56
5.1	Portrait of a Rescuer: Johannes Bogaard	70
5.2	British Diplomats and the *Kristallnacht*	80
6.1	Portrait of a Resister: Eta Wrobel	101
7.1	Liberation in the East	119

PREFACE

The Holocaust—the attempt by the Nazi regime of Germany to remove and then exterminate the Jews of Europe between 1933 and 1945—is arguably one of the most discussed topics of recent history. Writing about it is a massive assignment in view of the need for precision and, at the same time, comprehension. My hope is that in this short book I have been successful in managing to contextualize and explain the major contours of that terrible event.

The book is intended as a teaching tool as well as a volume to be read by a general audience—though much, it must be said, makes for depressing reading given its subject matter. Yet in addition to the horrors being recounted, there are stories of inspiration here as well, as we read of those who stood up to the Nazis and worked to thwart their destructive aims.

In seeking to provide a comprehensive introduction to the multifaceted phenomenon that was the Holocaust, I have been accompanied by the questions posed by my many students, in several institutions and levels on two continents, over the past three decades. The chapters in this book are a mirror of their concerns, and, I hope, will resonate with readers today.

There are two people to whom I must proffer my humble gratitude for their assistance in putting this small volume together. Each read every word in draft form, and each made valuable suggestions which enhanced the whole project in many ways. Michael Dickerman, with whom I had worked earlier on a major Holocaust encyclopedia project, brought his extraordinary editorial skills to the task, showing me along the way that his talents are many, varied, and immensely valuable.

Eve E. Grimm, with whom I have also published on aspects of the Holocaust, kept my writing honest and insisted that this was a project to which I could bring new understandings despite my own reservations.

A further vote of thanks is due to my publisher at Routledge, Dr. Eve Setch, who has been an exceptional guide from the time this project was first suggested as a complement to my earlier *Genocide: The Basics*. I have been blessed in being able to work with such a consummate and highly skilled professional. I also want to thank her assistant, Zoe Thomson, with whom I have just started working.

Writing a book of this length, on such a massive topic, has presented one major problem, which must be addressed here by way of a disclaimer; given the relative sizes of both the volume and the subject, there were only a limited number of areas it could cover. I have often found myself frustrated at not being able to introduce (much less develop) certain themes which, I am sure, some will say should have been explored here. With that in mind, I will only say this: the book you have in your hand is an introduction only, and makes no pretense at being the last word. Accordingly, I urge anyone holding it to go out and extend its boundaries—and do it now. It's never too late to make a better world.

Paul R. Bartrop
Fort Myers, Florida

INTRODUCTION
Defining the Holocaust

When looking at the Holocaust it is always advisable, as survivor Elie Wiesel has told us, to begin with tales. As he wrote in an essay as long ago as 1976:

> Let us tell tales. Let us tell tales—all the rest can wait, all the rest must wait.
>
> Let us tell tales—that is our primary obligation. Commentaries will have to come later, lest they replace or becloud what they mean to reveal.
>
> Tales of children so wise and so old. Tales of old men mute with fear. Tales of victims welcoming death as an old acquaintance. Tales that bring man close to the abyss and beyond—and others that lift him up to heaven and beyond. Tales of despair, tales of longing. Tales of immense flames reaching out to the sky, tales of night consuming life and hope and eternity.
>
> Let us tell tales so as to remember how vulnerable man is when faced with overwhelming evil. Let us tell tales so as not to allow the executioner to have the last word. The last word belongs to the victim. It is up to the witness to capture it, shape it, transmit it and keep it as a secret, and then communicate that secret to others.
>
> (1976: 258)

The tale with which we can begin here relates to one of the greatest of Jewish historians, the Russian-born Jewish scholar Simon Dubnow. His is not a survivor's story.

During the World War II, the elderly Dubnow was living in Riga, Latvia. Given the opportunity to escape the fearsome potential that a German invasion might bring, he decided to remain where he was, determined not to flee and in so doing hand the Nazis a victory. A number of witnesses to his death were later to provide the following record of his last moments:

> When the Nazis entered Riga they evicted Dubnow from his home and seized his entire library. They summoned him for questioning at Gestapo headquarters and then placed him in a home for the aged. After a short period of ghetto organization the Nazis liquidated the ghetto at the end of October 1941 and a month later they carried out their first "action" against the Riga Jews. Dubnow was seriously ill, but friends managed to conceal him for a while. On the night of December 7–8 the Nazis carried out their second "action." All the old and sick as well as the women in advanced pregnancy were herded together in buses. Dubnow was also taken outside to be squeezed into one of these overloaded buses. He was in a high fever at the time and was hardly able to move his feebled legs. A Latvian militiaman then advanced and fired a bullet in Dubnow's back and the sainted martyr fell dead on the spot. The next day several friends buried him in the old cemetery in the Riga ghetto. A story went round that the last words that Dubnow muttered as he was being led out to the bus were: "Brothers, don't forget! Recount what you hear and see! Brothers, make a record of it all!"
>
> (Pinson, 1970: 39)

This is the kind of story with which most survivors of the Holocaust could readily identify. All are driven by Dubnow's exhortation to remember and recount, and in doing so, to bear witness.

How are we to approach the enormous topic that is the Nazi Holocaust of the Jewish people? It negated every positive achievement of the twentieth century, a genocidal explosion that saw a sudden and irrevocable break with all the humanistic traditions that had been developing in Europe over the previous thousand years. The relationship between mass death and the industrial state that became manifested in the Holocaust was intimate, and as a result of it having taken place we forever have a yardstick by which all other cases of genocide must be measured. Its message is so powerful that no definition of Western civilization can ever again be constructed without reference being made to where the corruption of that civilization can lead.

The period of National Socialist rule across Europe was a time of immense upheaval, occasioned by deliberate and massive political violence. At first confined to Germany, it then spread to Austria, Czechoslovakia, and, eventually, to most of Europe. Its brutality was, until 1938, almost exclusively directed against political opponents, but by the end of the 1930s it began targeting Jews solely because of their Jewish identity.

The SS, the Nazi organization responsible for planning and executing the antisemitic measures, sought the elimination of those who it considered posed a threat through their very existence. This would be a genocidal struggle, forming part of a much broader campaign that also intended to destroy communism, wipe out the free-thinking opposition, and (after the onset of war) reduce the status of the population in the occupied areas (particularly in Eastern Europe) to that of ignorant and impotent vassals or serfs.

For the Nazis' aims to be realized, their leader, Adolf Hitler, needed the expertise of professionals capable of organizing the murder of vast numbers of people, as well as a bureaucracy comprised of men and women capable of implementing it. Hitler was able to call on the experts responsible for his ambitious pre-war eugenics scheme, which had seen the death of scores of thousands of so-called "defective" humans—Germans whom the Nazis referred to as having "life unworthy of life" with congenital illnesses, psychological problems, crippling injuries, or physical deformities, among other features distinguishing them from supposedly "normal" people. The experts responsible for killing these people had developed both the techniques and the mindset necessary for murdering large numbers of human beings. Adapting what they had already been doing to the much larger tasks required in Eastern Europe seemed, for many, to be a natural progression.

By 1941 the primary objective of Nazism had become the physical elimination of all of Europe's Jews. As one survivor of Auschwitz, Fania Fénelon, was later to recall, "The behavior of the SS was ruled by the terrible phrase: 'Woe to those who forget that everything that resembles a human being is not necessarily a human being'" (1977: 97–98).

The war ended in 1945, and the world that had been fought for by the democracies had been saved. With Nazism destroyed, optimism for the future was high. This excitement would be short-lived as the Cold War developed, but there was reason to hope that the postwar world would bring with it the realization of all liberal democracy's best ideals. One of several measures to bring this about, adopted by the newly established United Nations in 1948, was international legislation to prevent and punish the crime of genocide.

At that time there seemed to be no difficulty for people to identify it for what it was. A vast number of Europeans, in particular, already instinctively knew about genocide, even if the name was not yet in broad usage. In Allied capitals around the world, reports through both official channels and the media had already been conveying for some time the realities of the Nazi Holocaust, as evidence of the worst expressions of inhumanity was uncovered by liberating forces.

The genocidal nature of the Nazi regime is now such an established fact that it would not seem to require further elaboration. It was, it might be argued, the paradigmatic genocide (Garber, 1994). The perpetrators of the Holocaust had but one aim in mind: the complete removal of all Jews falling under their rule. An alteration of status through religious conversion or naturalization would not change their fate; in the Nazi view, every Jew, by virtue of his or her very birth, "was the static expression of Evil … a natural-born, predestined, non-assimilable heretic, doomed to Apocalyptic hellfire" (Rousset, 1951). The fate of the Jews was planned as a total annihilation, from which none would be allowed to escape. The Nazis intended nothing less than the physical destruction, through murder, of every Jew who fell into their net.

One of the questions often asked about the Holocaust, given its enormity, is whether or not it was unique within the annals of history (Rosenbaum, 2018). This, perhaps, is the wrong question. All historical phenomena are unique in that they will never again occur in exactly the same way or according to the time-and-place circumstances in which the original event happened. Every genocidal act of the past century, from the Hereros to the Armenians to the Ukrainians, from East Timor to Burundi to Cambodia to Rwanda to Bosnia to Darfur, has been characterized by specific developments which cannot be transferred from one setting to another—if only for the reason that human affairs do not act that way. The best that objective historians can hope to identify is the features that are common or different, and from this ascertain whether some sort of general pattern can be discerned.

As all cases of genocide have elements that are indeed unique unto themselves, the key question about the Holocaust should not be "was it unique?," but rather, turning the issue upside down, ask "what *was* unique about it?"—in other words, to assume its uniqueness and thereafter move straight on to identifying the feature or features that define its specific character.

To develop this discussion, we can take one aspect of the Holocaust—probably the most important of them all—the massive killing and destruction the Nazis inflicted on the Jews of Europe. The means they employed to achieve their murderous aims, especially from early 1942 onwards, was of course the death (or extermination) camp (*Vernichtungslager*), and it is this institution, thoroughly unprecedented in purpose and design, that is arguably the starkest feature of the Holocaust from 1942 onwards (Wachsmann, 2015).

Nothing, either before or since, approximates the Nazi death camps in design, intention, or operation. Nowhere have any other regimes producing malevolent concentration camps introduced establishments like these, in particular the "Operation Reinhard" death camps of Treblinka, Bełżec, and Sobibór. They were, and remain, thoroughly unprecedented in human history (Arad, 1987).

The period of National Socialist rule in Europe was a time of immense upheaval and dislocation, occasioned by deliberate and massive political violence. Its most extreme brief was to wage a genocidal struggle against the Jews, which, under the direction of Heinrich Himmler and Reinhard Heydrich, the SS undertook with what can best be described as a religious zeal. A vast array of different types of concentration camps evolved, with at least forty-three different categories existing at the height of the Nazis' power.

All of these institutions, whether concentration or extermination camps, were places of unmitigated horror, where life was characterized by "hard work, poor diet, over-crowded and unsanitary living conditions, and SS cruelty" (Edelheit and Edelheit, 1994: 67). Death by beating, bullets, or other means lurked around every corner. Throughout the war years, disease and starvation were constant companions. Deprived of all rights, ordinary inmates were subjected to the caprice of Nazi guards and the other prisoners placed in positions of authority over them.

The six death camps located in Poland—Auschwitz-Birkenau, Bełżec, Chełmno, Majdanek, Sobibór, and Treblinka—transformed the nature and course of Nazi concentration camp development. They were a departure from anything previously visualized in both their design and character, planned to methodically and efficiently murder millions of people, specifically Jews. They became the most lucid and unequivocal statement National Socialism made about itself, demonstrating beyond doubt that it was an anti-human ideology in which respect for life counted for nothing.

An understanding of the concentration and death camp system can add to our knowledge of Nazism in two important ways. First, it shows how a regime dedicated to mass murder mobilized all its resources for the purpose of feeding the demands of an industry that had been deliberately assigned the tasks of incarceration, degradation, and annihilation. Second, the history and fate of the camps demonstrates that the regime was aware that its activities were of a criminal and morally repugnant nature. After all, the Nazis chose to carry out their murderous assignments in places far removed from key population centers, accompanied by an exhaustive effort to destroy as much evidence of the killing as possible prior to being overrun by the advancing Allied forces. Put together, these aspects of what the death camps represented added up to a new dimension of inhumanity.

Millions of people suffered and died as a direct result of Nazi actions during World War II, but only the Jews were murdered because of the "crime" of their very existence (Berkowitz, 2007). Only the Jews were intended for total, complete, and utter annihilation, in which they would become extinct as a people. Why, therefore, does the Holocaust still matter? Because ignorance will triumph, and hatred, intolerance, bigotry, discrimination and thuggery will again become fashionable if it is forgotten. The passions unleashed against the Jewish people between 1933 and 1945 are the same kind that are still being unleashed against others, today. In our own self-interest, we must remember what happened, and take careful note, because, it might be argued, we dare not forget.

DISCUSSION QUESTIONS

- When speaking about the "Holocaust," what time period are we referring to?
- Why were the Jews singled out for extermination?
- What were the distinctive features of the Holocaust?
- Is it possible to define the Holocaust without reference to the Nazi campaign of annihilation against the Jews of Europe? Why/Why not?

OUTLINES, ORIGINS, AND CONSEQUENCES

OVERVIEW

The Holocaust is the term in English most closely identified with the attempt by Germany's National Socialist regime, in conjunction with its European allies, to exterminate the Jews of Europe during the period of World War II—particularly during its most destructive phase between 1941 and 1944. While an exact number of those murdered is impossible to determine, the best estimates settle at a figure approximating around six million Jews, one million of whom were children under the age of 12, and another half million of whom were aged between 13 and 18 (Laqueur, 2001).

The term "Holocaust" is most commonly used to describe the event, but two other terms are also employed, particularly within the Jewish world. The Hebrew word *Churban*, or "catastrophe," which historically has been employed to describe the destruction of the two Temples in Jerusalem, is one of these; the other, utilized increasingly, is the Hebrew term *Shoah* ("calamity," or, sometimes, "destruction").

The first step on the road to the Holocaust took place on the night of February 27–28, 1933, when the Reichstag building in Berlin, the home of the German parliament, was deliberately set on fire. Who was responsible for the arson has long been a matter of dispute (Hett, 2014), but the next day, on the pretext that it had been set by communists and that a left-wing revolution was imminent, newly appointed Chancellor Adolf Hitler prevailed upon President Paul von Hindenburg to sign an emergency proclamation entitled the Decree for the Protection of the People and the State. It suspended all the basic civil and individual liberties guaranteed under the Weimar Constitution, empowering the government to take such steps as necessary to ensure that what was touted as a threat to German society was removed. In the first few days hundreds were detained, with tens of thousands more in succeeding weeks.

Then, on March 20, 1933, *Reichsführer-SS* Heinrich Himmler announced the establishment of the first compound for political prisoners, about 15 kilometers northwest of Munich, on the outskirts of the town of Dachau (Dillon, 2015). Other camps soon followed, among them Oranienburg, Papenburg, Esterwegen, Kemna, Lichtenburg, and Börgermoor (Wachsmann, 2015).

These camps were originally places of political imprisonment, and were nicknamed "Wilde-KZ" ("wild concentration camps"), alluding to the fact that they sprang up like wildflowers after refreshing rain following a long period of drought. There was little in the way of planning or procedure, and the camps frequently operated without any apparent system or direction. Often, the very location of these places was impromptu. Dachau was a former gunpowder factory; Oranienburg was originally a brewery (and later, a foundry); and Börgermoor and Esterwegen were initially simply rows of barracks set down on open expanses of marshy heathland. In other camps, prisoners had to build their own housing, and started their camp life living in tents.

It is important to note that these camps were originally places for political prisoners. Captives were selected by using political criteria, the intention being to isolate political opposition and frighten the population into accepting Nazi rule—the regime itself viewed the incarceration of communists and related enemies as a form of punishment which by necessity had to be imposed on these political "criminals." Opponents, whether real, presumed, or potential, would be scared into submission (Sofsky, 1997). The only thing the Nazis demanded was political compliance. In their most basic sense the camps removed political opposition from the midst of the community, and intimidated the population into accepting the Nazi regime.

Initially Jews had been arrested for "transgressing" within the framework of the existing political classifications, but from 1935 onwards they were frequently being victimized for their Jewishness alone (Wünschmann, 2015). This was brought about by the so-called Nuremberg Laws on Citizenship and Race, which defined and put into practice the formal status of Jews in the Nazi state, and by which Jews were increasingly excluded from participation in all forms of German life. Jewish businesses were boycotted, Jewish doctors excluded from public hospitals and only permitted to practice on other Jews, Jewish judicial figures were dismissed and disbarred, Jewish professors were removed from their teaching posts and their Jewish students were expelled from universities. The Nuremberg Laws also withdrew from Jews the privilege of German citizenship. It became illegal for a Jew and a non-Jew to marry or engage in sexual relations. In short, life was to be made so intolerable that Jews would seek to emigrate; men who did not often found themselves arbitrarily arrested and sent to concentration camps. These arrests did not become widespread until 1938, and in most cases the victims were only held for a short time. The aim was to terrorize them into leaving the country (Schleunes, 1970).

The first large-scale arrests of Jews were made on and after the night of November 9–10, 1938, as "reprisals" for the assassination of consular official Ernst vom Rath by Jewish student Herschel Grynszpan in Paris a few days earlier. The event precipitating these arrests has gone down in history through use of the Nazi term for the episode, *Kristallnacht*, the "Night of Broken Glass" (Gilbert, 2007b). The resultant rampage was portrayed as a righteous and spontaneous outpouring of anger by ordinary German people against all Jews, even though for the most part it was Nazis in plain clothes who whipped up most of the action in the streets. The pogrom resulted in greater concentrated destruction than any previous anti-Jewish measure under the Nazis. By their own figures, 91 Jews had been killed and over 30,000 arrested and taken into "protective custody" (*Schutzhaft*) in concentration camps and prisons. Over 267 synagogues and 7,000 Jewish businesses were either destroyed or damaged. The real figures for all the destruction and lives lost were almost certainly higher, as many of the excesses went unrecorded. As a further insult, Nazi leader Hermann Göring ordered that the Jewish community be fined one billion Reichsmarks for the murder of vom

Rath, and a further six million Reichsmarks in insurance payments were to be paid to the government for "damages" to the German state (Thalmann and Feinermann, 1974). Jews who had up to now thought the regime was a passing phenomenon realized that this was not the case; tens of thousands now began looking for ways to leave Germany, by any means possible.

After *Kristallnacht*, within Germany Jews were targeted for the sole reason of their Jewishness: beforehand, Nazi persecution was not premised on acts of wanton destruction or murder, but the November pogrom had the effect of transforming earlier legislative measures against Jews into physical harassment on a broader and more indiscriminate scale than ever before. From then on, physical acts of an antisemitic nature became state policy. While Germany's Jews began frantically seeking sanctuaries to which they could emigrate in order to save their lives, the Free World began to close its doors to Jewish immigration (Dwork and van Pelt, 2009). Further, with Hitler's foreign policy appetite growing and new areas becoming annexed to the Third Reich (that is, Austria, the Sudetenland, "rump" Czechoslovakia, and Memel), the number of Jews coming under Nazi control increased to less manageable proportions.

The outbreak of war on September 1, 1939, saw the establishment of a system of ghettos in occupied Poland from October 1939 onwards, in order to segregate and confine Poland's Jewish population. Here, they were persecuted and terrorized, starved, and deprived of all medical care.

During the Nazi assault on the Soviet Union beginning in June 1941, mobile killing squads known as *Einsatzgruppen* ("Special Action Groups"), accompanying the German military, had been at work murdering all Jews found within their areas of command and control. The initial means by which they operated was to round up their captive Jewish populations—men, women, and children—take them outside of village and town areas, force the victims to dig their own mass graves, and then shoot them. When the repetition of that activity proved psychologically troublesome, mobile gas vans using carbon monoxide poisoning were brought in both to remove the intimacy of contact and sanitize the process. While at times technologically inefficient, from an economic perspective it was cost-effective in the use of both men and *materiél*. It is estimated that between 1941 and 1943 the *Einsatzgruppen* were responsible for the death of more than one million Jews (Rhodes, 2002; Desbois, 2008).

It is not known precisely when the decision to exterminate the Jews of Europe was made, though best estimates settle on sometime in the late summer or early fall of 1941 (Browning, 2004). At a conference held at Wannsee, Berlin, on January 20, 1942, the process was systematized and coordinated among Nazi Germany's relevant government departments (Roseman, 2002), and in the following months the Nazis established several camps in Poland for the express purpose of killing much larger numbers. From the summer of 1942 onwards the ghettos began to be liquidated, with the Jews sent to one of six death camps located throughout Poland. These six camps—Auschwitz-Birkenau, Bełżec, Chełmno, Majdanek, Sobibór and Treblinka—were a departure from anything previously visualized, in both their design and character. With the exception only of Auschwitz (which served simultaneously as a death camp, concentration camp, and labor camp complex), they were different from all others in that they did not perform any of the functions—political, industrial, agricultural, or penal—attributed to those further west or north. These were the *Vernichtungslager*, the death (or extermination) camps (see Box 2.1).

BOX 2.1 A CHILD'S EXPERIENCE: SHIRLEY BERGER GOTTESMAN

In April 1944 Shirley Berger Gottesman, a 16-year-old girl from Záluž, in Transcarpathian Poland/Ukraine, was deported to a ghetto in nearby Munkács, Hungary, along with her parents and four siblings. Soon after, they were sent to Auschwitz. Just a few hundred yards from the gas chambers and crematoria at Birkenau was an area of the camp the inmates called *Kanada*. Comprised of thirty barrack blocks transformed into storehouses northwest of the Auschwitz main camp, this nickname was given because the Poles in the camp saw the country of Canada as a land of great plenty and riches. In the barracks, inmates sorted and packaged new arrivals' belongings. These items were deposited in huge warehouses according to their type, after which they would be baled or boxed and then sent back to Germany.

This was where, in early June 1944, Shirley was sent to work and told to sort the possessions brought from arriving freight cars of Jews (termed "cattle cars" by the inmates). Upon her arrival, she recalled, she could not grasp what was happening, but after a short while, describing later the horror of what she witnessed, she stated that: "It was so unbelievable. I can't even conceive of what they did. Impossible! We were ready for work. We were even ready not to have enough food. We were not ready to be gassed."

Noting that long lines of people went into Crematoria III and IV—but that none ever came out—she was told by those who had been there longer than her that everybody not selected for work was gassed and burned. Upon coming to grips with this reality, she related, two crematoria were on one side; two on the other side, and that when the prisoners in her unit went to work they had to go between the crematoria: "We could see inside. Near the crematoria the grass was nicely kept—green. I saw chimneys. The fumes were terrible, especially in the summer. The odor of burning flesh! *Years after, when I smelled burning, I would scream.*"

Shirley's narrative offers eyewitness testimony of the gas chambers and the crematoria, from one who was only yards away from both for an extended period of time. It recorded the passive, resigned, almost stupefied sense with which the victims of the gas would approach their fate, seemingly without any sense of comprehension as to what was about to befall them. Her memoir was both a crucial statement of witness, and also that of a survivor who, in innumerable ways, suffered brutal psychological torture as a result of working in such a horrific environment, day after day, for months on end (Gottesman and McLoughlin, 2011; Bartrop, 2014).

The death camps were institutions designed to methodically and efficiently murder millions of Jews. The mass murders took place in specially designed gas chambers, employing carbon monoxide from diesel engines (either in fixed installations or from mobile vans), or crystallized hydrogen cyanide which on contact with air oxidized to become hydrocyanic (or prussic) acid gas. This was marketed by its commercial name, Zyklon B.

Notwithstanding that the Nazi armies on the Eastern Front began to retreat before the advancing Soviet forces (and later, after June 1944, from American and British troops in the west), renewed efforts were made at annihilating Jews while there was still time. Then, in March 1944, a shock of cataclysmic proportions fell upon the Jews of Hungary, the last great center of European Jewish population still untouched by the Holocaust. More than 400,000 Jews were murdered in the space of four months, with the killing facilities working non-stop, day and night. This was the fastest killing operation of any of the Nazi campaigns against Jewish populations in occupied Europe (Braham, 2000).

When viewing the Hungarian campaign and the means employed to attain it, it should be noted that Bełzec, Treblinka, Sobibór, and Chelmno had by this time already been evacuated. Only Auschwitz remained available to carry out the massive undertaking of spring 1944, as April had already seen the start of the evacuation of Majdanek. With the Soviet armies continuing their advance towards Germany throughout the latter half of 1944 the future of Auschwitz itself seemed uncertain, and the complete evacuation of the complex was ordered for January 17, 1945. The earliest date of free contact with Soviet forces was January 22, 1945; when the Auschwitz site was formally occupied two days later, there were only 2,819 survivors left (Strzelecki, 2008).

Prisoners still alive in the eastern camps at the end of the war were evacuated by the Nazis so as not to fall into the hands of the advancing Russians. These evacuations are known as death marches, as vast numbers of prisoners died or were killed whilst en route to their unknown destination away from the euphemistically named "east." Evidence that the Nazis tried to keep their prisoners alive is scant; prisoners who did not make it to their intended destination further west were treated with the same contempt as they would have been had they remained in the camp. Evacuated in the winter and early spring of 1944–1945, detainees had to contend with bitter cold, fatigue, hunger, and the SS guards themselves, as well as their own debilitated condition; for those who had already reached the limit of their endurance the death marches could have only one result. For others, the experience represented yet another challenge which had to be overcome. Often, the Russians were so close while the prisoners were marching away that the sounds of battle could be clearly distinguished, further adding to their distress. When the captives arrived at their new destination their trials were hardly eased, as they faced massive overcrowding in the camps to which they had been evacuated (Blatman, 2011).

The prisoners, dropped into places like Bergen-Belsen to await liberation through death or an Allied victory, actually had little time to wait, though each day dragged by unendingly. Painfully slowly, as German units both west and east surrendered, the camps were liberated. On April 12, 1945, Westerbork, in the Netherlands, was set free. Within Germany, Buchenwald's inmates rose against their SS guards and took over the camp on April 11, handing it to the Americans on April 13. Belsen was liberated by the British Army on April 15, and on April 23 the SS transferred the Mauthausen camp in Austria to the International Committee of the Red Cross. On April 24, Dachau was overrun by the U.S. Army. Five days later, on April 29, Ravensbrück was liberated. Theresienstadt, in Czechoslovakia, was handed over to the Red Cross by the Nazis on May 2, and on May 8 American troops occupied Mauthausen—the last major camp to be liberated in the west (Stone, 2015).

CAUSES OF THE HOLOCAUST

The historical background leading to the Holocaust is multifaceted, and for many years scholars have been grouped as being either "intentionalists" or "functionalists" (Lawson, 2010; Stone, 2010). The former grouping includes those who see the Holocaust as an event primarily centered in the person of Adolf Hitler, his antisemitism, and his commitment to bringing to realization a world "cleansed of Jews" (*Judenrein*). Functionalists, on the other hand, argue that the Holocaust was not the result of a planned, carefully organized, or orchestrated agenda from Hitler, but was, instead, an evolving and sometimes even chaotic program of death and destruction which really began to assert itself only after the invasion of Soviet Russia in June, 1941— prior to which it was undertaken in a somewhat haphazard and inefficient manner. A third strand of historians falls somewhere in the middle of the two camps, acknowledging and building their own interpretations on the strengths of each of the other groups' perspectives.

The roots of the Holocaust were very long. Nazi antisemitism built on a much longer-lasting hatred of the Jews as a people and also of Judaism as a religious tradition. The origins of anti-Jewish antipathy can be traced back to the Hebrew Bible, but with the birth and success of Christianity, and the New Testament's orientation of the Jews as being primarily responsible for the death of Jesus, antisemitism took on a religious expression (Wistrich, 2010). By the Middle Ages, the violence of religious antisemitism saw Crusades, pogroms, and persecutions based on the false charge that the deicide Jews needed to murder innocent Christian children to drain their blood for the preparation of unleavened bread during Passover, as well as the charge that the Jews poisoned wells resulting in the Black Death which ravaged Europe during the middle of the fourteenth century (Wistrich, 2010). While throughout much of European Christendom Jews were demonized for their religion, this does not however explain the Holocaust: in most cases, conversion to Christianity spared Jewish converts from any further harassment.

Along with being forbidden from owning and farming land, the rise of mercantilism and capitalism in Europe left unconverted Jews, who could not join guilds, as economic (as well as religious) outsiders. The secularization of civil society accompanying the European Enlightenment, along with a waning of the Church's power, brought new forms of social and political antisemitism to the fore.

The ultimate expression of antisemitism, which saw Jews as a biological category and Jewish identity as innate, created the preconditions for the most virulent and violent expression of antisemitism: the racial antisemitism of the Nazis.

For many people, the roots of the Holocaust lay in the impact of the Versailles Peace Conference of 1919, signed by a defeated Germany and the victorious allies of France, Britain, and the United States on June 28, 1919. The treaty required Germany to surrender Alsace-Lorraine, Eupen and Malmedy, Northern Schleswig, Holstein, West Prussia, Posen, Upper Silesia, the Saar, Danzig, and Memel; reduce its standing army to only 100,000 men; give up its naval and air forces; admit to full responsibility and guilt for the war; and pay massive reparations.

Adolf Hitler referred to Versailles as a "*Diktat*"—a dictated, not a negotiated, peace—and was motivated to utilize the document as one of the primary arguments for revenge against Jews, communists, socialists, and others who, he said, not only contributed to Germany's defeat in 1918, but were primarily responsible for the country's continuing social, political, economic, and military devastation during the years before he became German Chancellor in 1933. In large part, Hitler looked at Versailles as an instrument of "world Jewry's" attempt to reduce Germany to a vassal state. This, added to the general antisemitism that preceded Hitler's ascent to office, provided an important outlet for his racial views of the world.

In this context, ideology must be considered. The following essential features of Nazism, in particular, stand out: racial antisemitism; Social Darwinism and eugenics, in which civilization could be understood as an ongoing struggle for the survival of the fittest and most adaptable, coupled with a process of selective breeding of the human species; a mythical understanding of the German people (the "*Volk*"); the *Volk's* inherent right to integrate those populations which are truly Germanic (i.e. "Aryan"); and to occupy by right the land required for the *Volk's* growth, expansion, and the creation of a unique community (Bracher, 1970). The bedrock upon which these ideas rested was racism, which viewed the world in terms of superior and inferior human groups. Most of the "inferior" group had only one function—to serve the former. The exception was the Jews, who had no place in the Nazi new order.

The Jewish presence was considered a racial problem of the first magnitude. The only way to resolve it was to arrange for the total disappearance of Jews from Germany (and later, from Europe). Different solutions were proposed: voluntary emigration; forced emigration; and a variety of plans for deportation—to "the east," to Poland, to Siberia, to the island of Madagascar. All these plans had to be dropped, however, owing to the outbreak of war in 1939.

The Nazis had already gained experience with systematic mass murder in the form of the so-called Euthanasia (*Aktion T4*) Program (Aly, Chroust, and Pross, 1994). According to this, Germans with physical and psychological disabilities were murdered by the state in the name of biological "purity." Later, during World War II, this quest would be translated into outright extermination.

Finally, the suffering of the German people during the Depression, which led to massive hardship and poverty throughout the country, permitted the transference of blame by the Nazis onto the Jews as a minority who were disproportionately represented in the professions, providing them with greater wealth and access to privilege.

The process of massive industrial-scale killing really began only after Operation Barbarossa, the German invasion of the Soviet Union on June 22, 1941 (Glantz, 2009; Stahel, 2009). The invasion was accompanied by a *Führerbefehl* (Führer Order) from Hitler in which he reinforced his often-proclaimed role of Savior of Europe against Bolshevism. Prior to Barbarossa, on June 6, 1941, Hitler issued his *Kommissarbefehl* (Commissar Order), in which he directed that any captured Soviet cadres or political leaders would be summarily executed. By extension, within the Nazi conception of communism, this included all Jews, as they were viewed as the chief disseminators of Bolshevik ideology. The mobile killing squads, the *Einsatzgruppen* ("Special Action Groups"), were established specifically to accompany the combat troops of the German Army close behind in the weeks following the invasion (Rhodes, 2002; Desbois, 2008), and while this was not in itself one of the causes of the Holocaust, it nonetheless precipitated the massive murderous actions that were to have their greatest expression in the death camps established by the Nazis in Poland during 1942.

Overall, it can be said that some of the more important causes of the Holocaust can be found in the long history of Christian religious antisemitism; the advent of political and racial antisemitism; Social Darwinism; extreme nationalism; totalitarianism; industrialization; and the nature of modern war. Adolf Hitler and the

Nazis implemented the measures that we know as the Holocaust, but this raises more questions than it answers. Hitler was the driving force behind the obsessive and fanatical Nazi persecution, and ultimately also the mass slaughter of the Jews: but he could not achieve his ambitions alone. In order to learn what allowed Hitler and his party to implement their ideas, regard must always be given to the deeper causes.

CONSEQUENCES OF THE HOLOCAUST

When reflecting the consequences of the Holocaust we must consider the enormous loss of life generated by Nazi rule. Owing to the industrialized and impersonal nature of Nazi mass murder, historians have found it difficult to provide a single, definitive figure of Jewish losses, though most estimates have settled at around 6 million of the 7.3 million Jews who inhabited the countries and regions of what became German-occupied Europe (Laqueur, 2001). These losses included the Jews of Poland (2.7 million), Hungary (559,250), the Netherlands (102,000), Romania (120,919), and the Soviet Union (2.1 million) (Laqueur, 2001).

Because the Nazis transported the majority of their victims from one place to another in order to murder them, the names of some localities will forever be associated with mass annihilation and human destruction—most importantly, the six death camps established by the Nazis in Poland referred to earlier.

The loss of two-thirds of European Jewry, representing more than one-third of the world's Jews in 1939, led to devastating results from which the global Jewish population has not yet recovered. In 1939, there were 17 million Jews in the world, and by 1945 only 11 million. The loss of so many lives deprived the world of generations unborn, talent that did not see realization, and contributions to civilization that were never made. Most of the survivors, particularly in Eastern European countries, found they did not have homes to which they could return. Not only had their countries been devastated by the war, but in many cases they were not welcomed back into their original communities.

As a result, the Holocaust impacted the European Jewish community long after the killing stopped, as it ended communal life that in some cases stretched back well beyond a thousand years. The war left 250,000 displaced Jews languishing in camps awaiting a new home. While a new dispersal out of Europe took place, the Holocaust also served to hasten the return of Jewish populations to the Jews' ancestral homeland in Palestine, which by 1948 had become the independent Jewish state of Israel. An important consequence of the Holocaust thus saw an end—in part—of the Jewish Diaspora in Europe. The distribution of the global Jewish population now is completely different from what it was before World War II. Europe, where the Jewish presence was thoroughly devastated, gave way to Israel and the United States as the new major centers of Jewry.

Beyond the killing, the Holocaust had other consequences affecting the way in which people thought about the very nature of the human condition. Prior to the Holocaust, the Nazi belief in racial eugenics, the "science" advocating the use of practices aimed at improving the genetic composition of a population, was a given. *Rassenhygiene* (as it was termed in German) was understood to mean the improvement of the human species through selective breeding and the elimination of those hereditary factors that "weakened" a species. By the time Nazis assumed power in 1933, they were able to apply such ideas to so-called "racial" categories, specifically Jews and Roma. Nazi scientists and propagandists were thereafter able to "prove" the inferiority of non-Aryan peoples, and thus lay the groundwork for their ultimate extermination. After the Holocaust, notions of eugenics and racial superiority were thoroughly discredited. Ideas of racial antisemitism were exposed as thoroughly fallacious, and the thought that a "superior" race could be bred artificially was brought to an absolute end.

Another important consequence of the Holocaust came as a result of the very destruction itself. After six years of total war— and its accompanying massive loss of life—the Holocaust awakened the conscience of humanity, with the cry of "Never again!" raised everywhere, resulting in two important initiatives: the quest for post-Holocaust justice, and a search for ways to ensure that it could never recur.

At the end of the war, and in response to the revelations exposed with the liberation of the Nazi concentration camps, the Allies conducted the Nuremberg Trials between October 18,

1945, and October 1, 1946, involving the prosecution of twenty-two leading Nazis at the International Military Tribunal (Conot, 1983; Persico, 1994). Nuremberg was much more than simply a trial sitting in judgment on the perpetrators of the Holocaust (in fact, it was not convened for that purpose), as nothing was seen in the first instance as being more criminal than the Nazis having foisted a war of aggression upon a world which had previously been clearly committed to avoiding it. In the popular awareness, however, the Nuremberg Trials were viewed as judgment on the Holocaust, owing to the shocking revelations and film footage that came to light in evidence. The Charter of the Nuremberg Trials was unprecedented in international law, and a vital step on the road to a universal anti-genocide, anti-crimes against humanity, and anti-war crimes regime that would be binding upon all. This would see its crowning moment in 2002, with the institution of the International Criminal Court in The Hague.

In this sense, an important consequence of the Holocaust was the emergence of a worldwide civil rights movement after 1945. While the Nuremberg Trials came to an end in 1946, enshrining the principle of individual responsibility for war crimes and crimes against humanity, two other crucial legacies were instituted by the United Nations one day apart in December, 1948: the Convention on the Prevention and Punishment of the Crime of Genocide (December 9, 1948), and the Universal Declaration on Human Rights (December 10, 1948). With these, it seemed as though the world's conscience had learned an important lesson from the horror of the Holocaust, specifically, that its repetition would not be tolerated. Sadly, although an awakening such as this was long overdue, the message did not penetrate to all sectors of society, as the genocides of the second half of the twentieth century were to testify.

DISCUSSION QUESTIONS

- To what extent do you think the Holocaust can be described as "unique?"
- Did Hitler and the Nazis plan the annihilation of the Jews from the very beginning of the Third Reich, or was the "Final Solution" something that evolved gradually over time?

- What were the antisemitic measures instituted in the period 1933 to 1939, and why did the Nazis introduce them?
- What were the means employed in order to achieve the "Final Solution?"
- What were the major consequences of the Holocaust? Do any predominate over others?

PERPETRATORS OF THE HOLOCAUST

OVERVIEW

The Nazi Party controlled Germany from 1933 to 1945, and throughout that period it persecuted and murdered political opponents, Jews, homosexuals, Roma, Slavs, and German citizens with mental and physical disabilities. Despite a recent trend to include all those killed by the Nazis as victims of the Holocaust—thus leading some to refer to "11 million Holocaust victims"—the clearest definition of the Nazi terror lay in the deliberate attempt to annihilate every Jew who fell into the Nazi net. No other group was targeted in this way.

Who perpetrated these crimes? For the mother forced to choose between two children on the ramp at Auschwitz, it was the Nazi doctor forcing the choice; for the teenager torn from the embrace of her little sister because she was old enough to work while the younger girl was not, it was an SS officer; for the old man beaten to death by the side of the road by a Nazi soldier because he couldn't move fast enough when ordered to, it was that soldier; and for the newlyweds who were forced into the squalor of the ghetto where the bride watched her husband die of starvation and disease, only to die herself immediately afterward, the Holocaust was represented by those who had brought them into this condition.

Moreover, one did not have to be a German in order to implement Nazi actions. This was made clear through the experiences Jews had with the Arrow Cross (Nyilas) Party in Hungary, the Hlinka Guard in Slovakia, antisemitic Poles who denounced Jews to their German occupiers, Vichy French officials and police, Ukrainian collaborators, and so on. For many people who never saw a German, the Holocaust was visited upon them by a wide variety of messengers.

While an immediate response to the question of who perpetrated the Holocaust might settle on the person of Adolf Hitler, it must always be borne in mind that Hitler could not have achieved the destruction of European Jewry unaided. Within Nazi Germany all sectors of society played their role in planning, facilitating, and executing the Final Solution. They ranged from the major leaders of the Nazi Party—Hitler, Heinrich Himmler, Hermann Göring, Josef Goebbels, Reinhard Heydrich, and many others—through bankers, senior officers of the German Army, police, civil servants, university academics, railway men, chemists, doctors, journalists, engineers, and the judiciary. Not everyone was necessarily aware of the full impact of the role they were playing, but all fitted into the bigger picture, and few questioned what the logical outcome of their actions could be.

Perhaps the most important agent of death was the SS (*Schutzstaffel*), an arm of the Nazi Party formed in 1923 as a specialized unit of fifty men to act as Hitler's personal bodyguard (Weale, 2010). After Hitler's failed *putsch* of November 11, 1923, the SS was banned, but it was reconstituted under the leadership of Heinrich Himmler as a racially elitist unit in 1929. In its creation, Himmler conceived of a paramilitary organization consisting of men with high moral caliber, honesty, and decency, who would be committed to the Nazi vision and agenda and thoroughly antisemitic in their orientation. Its infamous black uniform and *Totenkopf* or "Death's Head" insignias were introduced in 1932. By 1933 it was a force of more than 200,000 men. Under Himmler's guidance, the SS not only developed the Nazi concentration camp system, but also took responsibility for staffing the camps, instituting the discipline policies within them, and planning how best to exploit the prisoners as slave labor.

From the summer of 1941 onwards, the SS took control of the annihilation of Europe's Jews, first through the *Einsatzgruppen* and then, after 1942, through the extermination camps located in Poland. Thus, those primarily responsible for the murder of European Jewry in the various slave labor, concentration, and death camps came from the ranks of the SS. After the war, at the International Military Tribunal at Nuremberg, the SS was formally declared a criminal organization, and disbanded. Himmler committed suicide, but the overwhelming majority of SS members were never brought to trial.

Many Nazis of high rank (though not Hitler or Göring), as well as many members of the SS, were well educated (Fest, 1970). Josef Goebbels held a PhD from the University of Heidelberg; Heinrich Himmler studied agronomy at the Munich *Technische Hochschule* (now the University of Technology, Munich); Hans Frank, appointed Governor-General of occupied Poland, was a lawyer, as were a majority of the fifteen attendees at the Wannsee Conference in January 1942 (Jasch and Kreutzmüller, 2017). Alfred Rosenberg, the Nazi Party's leading race ideologue, possessed a PhD in engineering from a university in pre-revolutionary Russia. Three out of the four commanders of the *Einsatzgruppen* operating in the Soviet Union had earned doctorates. The list goes on. All were integral to a genocidal project that formed a central platform of the Nazi state.

It was recognized after the war that many of those involved in the murder process had been keen to take part in the killing activities. The members of Reserve Police Battalion 101, which will be discussed later in this chapter, were among these, and form an important case study of how participation worked. In addition, throughout occupied Europe there were many ordinary people who enjoyed the power Nazi authority gave them, while others employed the situation for personal gain. Perpetrators and collaborators were to be found in every country, and the Nazis relied upon them to carry out their terrible acts against individuals and communities across Europe.

Ever since revelations about the Holocaust first came to light, questions have abounded regarding the nature of those who perpetrated what was, unquestionably, the greatest criminal act of deliberate mass murder in history. Did the killers not possess a conscience? Were they all psychopaths? What type of society was the Germany that could plan and carry out this massive criminal act?

To address these and other questions, many studies have been made of those whose actions describe them as perpetrators of the Holocaust, looking at the phenomenon from a variety of perspectives (Bartrop and Grimm, 2019). When all such studies are taken into consideration, however, certain facts remain constant—the primary one of which is that the Final Solution was a massive state project that was at the heart of Nazi wartime race and population policy.

It must be remembered that it was a *Nazi* government from *Germany* that was responsible for the Holocaust. Antisemitism was a primary building block of Nazism and featured prominently in the party platform of 1920. There was always a compulsion to eliminate Jews from German life, though it is important to realize that initially Nazism did not automatically equate with genocidal mass murder. This was an aspiration that developed over time, as did the techniques—and the expertise—to achieve it.

The destruction of the Jewish people was never the policy of any other European country or government. Adolf Hitler, as head of the Nazi government, was its instigator, and his views of the Jews as an "eternal race-enemy," coupled with his notions of inclusivity and exclusivity relating to the German *Volk*, could leave no-one with any illusions as to his preferences.

As noted earlier, however, Hitler could not have achieved his aims relative to the Jews (or anything else) without the willing (and often enthusiastic) support of others around him. The head of the SS, Heinrich Himmler, and those in charge of the security services, Reinhard Heydrich and Kurt Daluege, created a tyrannical police state founded on issues of race, control, and violence. And the SS was the foremost agency of security, surveillance, and terror both within Germany and, later, throughout German-occupied Europe. Members of the SS not only became the most important actors in the destruction of the Jews of Europe; the entire project was entrusted to Himmler and Heydrich and run as an SS campaign.

To implement this campaign, hundreds of thousands of people were directly involved in carrying out the Final Solution. The political leaders of the Third Reich were of course those who designed the entire operation, but the organizers and killers came from a variety of Nazi organizations. These were the elite guardians of mass murder, forming the essential personnel running the extermination camps, operating the *Einsatzgruppen*, and administering the whole program.

PROPAGANDA—CONDITIONING THE POPULATION FOR GENOCIDE

In order to carry it out, the Nazi regime required a cooperative population, and propaganda was one of the most important means by which this was achieved (Herf, 2006; Bachrach and Luckert, 2009).

Well before they came to power, Adolf Hitler and his followers were convinced that the Jewish people posed a deadly threat to humanity. They held that all their enemies were part of what they termed "international Jewry," and were convinced that Jews controlled the governments of the Soviet Union, the United Kingdom, and the United States. In the Nazi vision, Jews were represented as parasitic organisms—as leeches, lice, bacteria, or carriers of disease. Hitler's dehumanization of the Jews excluded them from the system of moral rights and obligations that bind humankind together.

Following the Nazi seizure of power in 1933, Hitler established a Reich Ministry of Public Enlightenment and Propaganda, headed by Joseph Goebbels (Welch, 1993). The Ministry's aim was to ensure that the Nazi message was successfully communicated through art, music, theater, films, books, radio, educational materials, and the press. Goebbels created various forms of propaganda showing different messages to publicize the Nazis and turn the people against the Jews. When combined with antisemitic feelings already prevailing in many parts of Europe, these resulted in violence, humiliation, and anti-Jewish persecution.

Hitler began shaping the beliefs of school children through the reading of assigned texts in which Jews were portrayed in a series of increasingly negative scenarios. The use of stereotyped conceptions of Jews as lecherous old men seducing young Aryan women and girls, unscrupulous lawyers, hard-hearted landlords, rich businessmen and their wives ignoring the poverty around them, all combined to create a hate-filled image of Jews. Supported by the government, Julius Streicher, editor of the weekly newspaper *Der Stürmer*, spread antisemitic propaganda to the general public throughout Germany (Bytwerk, 2001). The "facts" presented in his newspaper were carried over into schoolbooks. Streicher sought to create a perception of Jews as a subhuman race that was a threat to Germany. The idea was for the total indoctrination of these beliefs to such an extent that the population became convinced about the inferiority of Jews and the need to eliminate the threat they posed to the purity of the Aryan race.

Since not all Germans could travel to hear Hitler speak in person, Goebbels arranged for every household to obtain a cheap radio at a heavily subsidized price. Called Peoples' Receivers, citizens (but not Jews) were expected to use them to take advantage of Hitler's regular broadcasts to the German people.

Books became the object of propaganda, and not only through Hitler's own *Mein Kampf*, which was distributed free to newlywed couples and soldiers. The Ministry for Popular Enlightenment and Propaganda identified "degenerate literature" which was removed from university and public libraries. These volumes included anti-Nazi or communist works written by Jews or those sympathetic to Jews, and were subject to highly organized book burnings commissioned by the Ministry.

The cinema played an important role in disseminating racial antisemitism, the superiority of German military power, and the intrinsic evil of the enemies as defined by Nazi ideology (Welch, 1983). Nazi films portrayed Jews as "subhuman" creatures infiltrating Aryan society. For example in 1940 *Die Ewige Jude* (*The Eternal Jew*), directed by Fritz Hippler, portrayed Jews as wandering cultural parasites, consumed by sex and money. *Die Ewige Jude* prepared the German people for the removal of Jews, so that when the deportations began neighbors would associate Jews with rats or vermin, rather than see them as humans.

As the Final Solution was being carried out, SS officials at killing centers compelled their victims to maintain the deception needed to deport Jews from Germany and occupied Europe without resistance. These prisoners, many of whom would soon die in the gas chambers, were forced to send postcards home saying they were well and living in good conditions. The authorities used this misinformation as propaganda to cover up atrocities and mass murder.

The Nazi regime used propaganda effectively to mobilize the German population to support its wars of conquest until the very end of the regime. Propaganda was likewise essential to motivating those who implemented the mass murder of the European Jews and of other victims. It also served to secure the acquiescence of millions of others—as bystanders—to racially targeted persecution and mass murder. Eliminating their rights and freedoms, and driving

Jews into poverty and despair, Nazi propaganda created hatred against the Jews and set the stage for the genocide.

In a remarkable documentary made in 2005, Danish film maker Ove Nyholm sought to learn what the motivations of mass murderers were in a time of war. Interviewing Serbian killers from the Yugoslav wars of the 1990s, he showed how such men, through their actions, acquired ancestors—the SS murderers of the Holocaust. He was, he said, attempting to plumb the depths of heartlessness. Quoting one of the *Einsatzgruppen* killers who was confronted by a victim just before gunning them down in a pit killing, Nyholm reached what he considered to be the quintessential justification of genocide: "You must die," the SS officer said, "so that we might live" (2005).

Upon further reflection, Nyholm sought to ascertain just how extensive the killing culture was: the density, in real-world terms, of the murder cohort when charted on a map of Germany. He took the figure of 107,000 files relating to alleged Nazi war criminals held in the archives of the Central Office of the State Justice Administrations for the Investigation of National Socialist Crimes (*Zentrale Stelle der Landesjustizverwaltungen zur Aufklärung nationalsozialistischer Verbrechen*), in Ludwigsburg, Germany. Calculating the ratio of war criminals in relation to the total geographical area of the country (including lakes, mountains, and forests), he found an average of 2.4 perpetrators per square kilometer. "Seen from street level," he concluded, "that's less than 700 meters between each one; 688 meters, to be precise" (Nyholm, 2005).

AN ENVIRONMENT OF PERPETRATION

While shocking, this tells only part of the story, for there were many thousands of others involved for whom files were not kept. SS and police commanders, together with those commanding the *Einsatzgruppen*, directed the clearing of ghettos and villages, the concentration of inhabitants in open spaces, and then the systematic shooting of men, women, and children in the killing fields of the Soviet Union. In Poland, SS leaders established factories of death, killing centers equipped with gas chambers that enabled mass murder to take place as if on an assembly line.

And it was not only the SS and police who were actively enmeshed in the implementation of the Final Solution. Until a short time ago the German Army had, for several decades, projected the image that it was not directly caught up in the killing of Jews; its sole responsibility was always (so the argument went) one of military combat. More recent scholarship, however, has shown conclusively that the Wehrmacht made its contribution to the Final Solution in the Soviet Union, and that the SS did not act alone (Pasher, 2014). This involvement, it must be added, sometimes extended to the highest levels of the military, while letters and photographs sent home by frontline German soldiers often documented atrocities—either those they had witnessed, or those in which they had themselves taken part.

It is remarkable, moreover, how frequently many of the actual "coal-face" killers encountered each other throughout the war. Schooled in murder during the early days of the Nazi movement, they became experts in their craft and as experienced specialists they could often be found close by to each other—at meetings, in the camps, or in their numerous deployments. Indeed, often they succeeded each other in different assignments.

While an immediate response to the question of who was responsible for perpetrating the Holocaust might settle on the person of Adolf Hitler, it must always be borne in mind that within Nazi Germany all sectors of society played their role in planning, facilitating, and executing the Final Solution. Those who did nothing to act against what they saw of the Nazi actions on a daily basis were thereby complicit (see Box 3.1).

WHO ENABLED THE HOLOCAUST TO BE CARRIED OUT?

A broad cross-section of German society fits into the category of "Who made it possible." The Holocaust process was top-heavy with well-educated professionals: bankers, professors, doctors, journalists, engineers, judges, teachers, lawyers, and civil servants. The range of those who aided and abetted the killers was as wide-ranging as the German social fabric itself. Carrying out the Final Solution required cooperation from people in all walks of life.

Among the leaders in the corporate world were the owners and managers of major industrial and commercial enterprises who sought to profit from Nazi programs of Aryanization and persecution of the

BOX 3.1 PORTRAIT OF A PERPETRATOR: RUDOLF HOESS

Rudolf Franz Ferdinand Hoess (also spelled Höss) was commandant of Auschwitz between 1940 and 1943. He was born into a strict Roman Catholic family on November 25, 1900, in Baden-Baden, the only son of three children. His father wanted him to train for the priesthood, but he turned against Catholicism in his early teens after his priest reported to his father something Hoess had spoken about during confession.

With the onset of World War I, a 14-year-old Hoess tried three times join the Army, but on each occasion he was sent home. He then lied about his age at 15, and enlisted in his father's and grandfather's old regiment. He was posted to the Middle East Front, served in Turkey and Palestine, and at 17 became the Army's youngest non-commissioned officer. Wounded three times, he was awarded the Iron Cross and other military decorations.

After the war Hoess returned to Germany and completed his secondary education. Like many young veterans at a loose end, he joined a *Freikorps* group, and in early 1922 was first introduced to Adolf Hitler. Conservative, racist, and extremely nationalistic, he joined the Nazi Party the same year.

Fighting in the streets against communists and "traitors," Hoess and other *Freikorps* members (including Martin Bormann) were arrested in June 1923 after beating the local schoolmaster to death for handing over to France a "patriot" engaged in sabotage during the French occupation of the Ruhr. Hoess was sentenced to ten years' jail and remained in prison until July 1928.

He emerged from prison a hero. In 1929 he married Hedwig Hensel, and between 1930 and 1943 they had five children, who later lived with him at Auschwitz. On April 1, 1934, Hoess joined the SS; in December 1934 he was appointed as a block leader at Dachau concentration camp, where he was mentored by Theodor Eicke. In August 1938 he was transferred to Sachsenhausen, and in

1939, after the invasion of Poland, he joined the Waffen-SS. He performed his duties so well that in April 1940, when Heinrich Himmler created a new camp in Upper Silesia, he chose Hoess as its first commandant.

Thus, on May 1, 1940, Hoess was deployed to a prison camp consisting of old army barracks near the town of Auschwitz (Oświęcim). He had orders to devise a compound for 10,000 prisoners, and resolved to develop a camp more efficient than either Dachau or Sachsenhausen. The camp was already operational in June 1940, when the first 700 prisoners arrived.

During the three-and-a-half years in which Hoess commanded the camp, he developed the huge complex known as Auschwitz-Birkenau, consisting of three separate facilities on 8,000 hectares (20,000 acres), embracing a vast number of satellite sub-camps.

In June 1941, Hoess met with Himmler in Berlin and learned that Hitler had given the order for the mass murder of the Jews. Hoess said later Himmler had chosen Auschwitz as a killing site because of its isolation and easy rail access. Hoess was ordered to keep this information secret and was informed that Adolf Eichmann would be giving him all operational orders. Eichmann arrived at the camp four weeks later.

In October 1941, Hoess cleared a huge area around Auschwitz I and built a second camp, Auschwitz II, called Birkenau, which became the killing site. Hoess was closely involved in selecting the best methods for killing large numbers of people. He set up experiments in which a truck's exhaust fumes were piped back into a sealed cabin to asphyxiate those trapped inside, but finding that trucks took too long to kill large numbers of people he implemented gas chambers. Eventually he used a disinfectant, Zyklon-B, which killed faster and more thoroughly than exhaust fumes.

During standard camp operations, two to three trains carrying 2,000 prisoners each would arrive daily, for periods of four to six weeks. The prisoners were unloaded at

Birkenau; those fit for labor were marched to barracks either in Birkenau or one of the Auschwitz sub-camps, while those unsuitable for work went immediately to the gas chambers. At first, small gassing bunkers were located deep in the woods, to avoid detection. Later, four large gas chambers and crematoria were constructed at Birkenau to make the killing more efficient and to handle the increasing rate of extermination.

In May 1942 Hoess built a third camp, Auschwitz III, or Monowitz, to provide slave labor for German chemical firm I.G. Farben's synthetic rubber works, and later for other German industries. By 1943 Auschwitz was an enormous complex that at its height housed about 100,000 prisoners. It is estimated that 2.5 million people died there—mostly Jews, but also Roma, Soviet prisoners of war, and many other nationalities and ethnic groups.

Hoess lived at Auschwitz in a villa with his wife and children. He was a loving family man who returned to his home after completing his day's work at Auschwitz.

In December 1943 Hoess was rewarded for his efforts at Auschwitz with a promotion to Deputy Inspector of Concentration Camps under Richard Glücks, after which he traveled all over Germany inspecting and improving camp operations. As the German armies retreated across Europe he then began to arrange for the dismantling of some of the camps.

On May 8, 1944, Hoess returned to Auschwitz to supervise the destruction of the Jews of Hungary. Under his administration, 430,000 Jews were transported to the camp and killed in 56 days between May and July. Even Hoess's expanded facility could not handle the huge number of corpses, and the camp staff had to dispose of tens of thousands of bodies by burning them in open pits.

When Germany surrendered in May 1945 Hoess went into hiding. In March 1946 he was discovered and arrested. A witness at the trial of the major war criminals at Nuremberg, he was then turned over to the Polish government, who had demanded his extradition. He was tried for murder

> and various war crimes, and found guilty. He never denied what he did, but claimed to have simply been following orders. He was taken to Auschwitz, the scene of so many of his crimes, and hanged there on April 15, 1947 (Hoess, 1960; Bartrop, 2014).

Jews. Many of the major German corporations were running short of labor to carry out the day-to-day work in which they were engaged; they did not hesitate to use slave labor from concentration camp inmates who were being worked to death under extraordinarily brutal conditions. Nor could many of these same corporations resist theft—of ideas, premises, artwork, and client lists—from Jewish (or formerly Jewish) companies.

RESERVE POLICE BATTALION 101

After the war it was recognized that many people involved in the murder process had volunteered eagerly to be part of it. Others, however, always saw themselves as simply obeying orders, such as several members of Reserve Police Battalion 101, a unit of 500 middle-aged, lower- and lower-middle class family men from Hamburg, who were drafted into the aptly named "Order Police" and were active in murdering up to 38,000 men, women, and children in Eastern Europe in 1942 and 1943. Revelations about this unit were brought to light in a book published in 1992 entitled *Ordinary Men*, by historian Christopher Browning (1992), who employed the postwar court records of 210 former members to ascertain what drove the men in the unit to commit their crimes with such deadly effectiveness.

Browning's chilling conclusion was that these men—ordinary men from Hamburg, who had been drafted but found unfit for combat duty—were neither Nazi fanatics nor socio-pathological misfits. Within their cohort, Browning argued, the men often killed as a result of peer pressure and a fundamental obedience to authority. The broader implication of his study was that people do not have to be maladjusted individuals or political fanatics in order to commit mass murder, but that, rather, group pressure and comradeship plays an important role when it comes to obeying even the most horrific orders.

A variety of hypotheses were offered regarding their behavior: wartime brutalization; racism; segmentation and routinization of their tasks; careerism; obedience to authority and orders; ideological indoctrination; conformity; quasi-military status; and a sense of elitism. No single explanation, however, provided the answer. Moreover, as Browning showed, the case of Reserve Police Battalion 101 was not unique; its actions could certainly be extrapolated beyond this single unit.

The release of *Ordinary Men* caused considerable disquiet among those who had preferred to believe that there was something demonic in the Nazis that led them to committing atrocities during the Holocaust. Browning was the subject of sustained criticism from Harvard University scholar Daniel Goldhagen, whose alternative argument—that an innate German antisemitic culture caused the Holocaust—polarized the argument of why it was that Germans were so prepared to unleash the Holocaust on the Jews of Europe (1996). Goldhagen's own contribution to the discussion, a controversial book produced in 1996 entitled *Hitler's Willing Executioners*, was seen as the most logical response to *Ordinary Men*, though many scholars of the Holocaust thought it was a poor attempt at a rebuttal that did little to undermine Browning's essential position. *Ordinary Men*, on the other hand, received substantial praise from a majority of academic Holocaust experts.

DESK KILLERS

Some Nazis involved in the killing process rarely if ever moved out of their offices, yet were an integral part of the Holocaust nevertheless. Such a person was referred to by political philosopher Hannah Arendt as a "desk killer" (*Schreibtischtäter*) (Arendt, 1963). The term has come to be given to the process whereby bureaucrats administer policies of genocide that have been devised by politicians or military leaders. The most infamous desk killer was the Nazi civil servant Adolf Eichmann, who was given responsibility by his superior, Reinhard Heydrich, for devising the means and coordinating the process of deporting and transporting Jews to ghettos, labor camps and, ultimately, to the death camps located in Poland.

Eichmann threw himself into his work with enthusiasm. He saw himself as an effective administrator, dealing with a major policy issue that had been entrusted for resolution to his care. That it involved the murder of millions of people was of little concern; the important thing for him, in his bureaucratic capacity, was to deal with the task assigned to him (Arendt, 1963).

Other desk killers typically addressed their tasks in a similar vein; they were detached, deliberate, efficient, and highly focused on meeting their objectives without succumbing to the temptation of human morality that might deflect their attention. By doing their job as effectively as they were able, so the logic ran, they were sparing the victims harm and anxiety, at the same time helping the German people into the future. It was because of this approach that the desk killers often failed to see the criminal nature of their work—but it facilitated the Holocaust no less than the work of those on the front lines.

THE INFAMOUS SISTERHOOD: WOMEN AS PERPETRATORS

In 2013, extending work already undertaken by Elizabeth Harvey ten years earlier (2003), historian Wendy Lower brought the issue of women as perpetrators to a broad audience (2013). Each covered the actions of women in the killing process in Eastern Europe, exposing the extent to which women assisted not only in managing the Nazi actions but also in participating in settlement schemes in areas German conquest had taken over in the quest for *Lebensraum* ("living space"). Overlooked, however, was the role of women as guards, administrators, and perpetrators in the Nazi concentration camps. Indeed, when discussions take place regarding the brutality of guards in the concentration camps it is usual to consider male perpetrators in this role, with reference almost always made to "SS *men*." Yet as historian Christopher Dillon has pointed out, SS Chief Heinrich Himmler "was reluctant to deploy male SS personnel to guard female concentration camp prisoners" (2015: 214). From the outset, he notes, violence against women did not align with the masculinist ideals of the SS.

A female guard corps was, however, established at Lichtenburg camp in 1937, where they carried out the supervision of inmates.

This was carried over to Ravensbrück when Lichtenburg was closed, and the former camp was established for women in May 1939 (Helm, 2014).

Certain features can be discerned through examining the careers of several women who all knew and interrelated with each other and shared similar experiences and fates. Conclusions of a comparative nature can only be tentative, but similarities in their life trajectories, as we shall see, certainly exist.

Dorothea Binz was a guard at Ravensbrück, where she gained a reputation as one of the most brutal women within the Nazi system (Brown, 2002; Adele and Sarti, 2011). With beautiful blonde hair and blue eyes, she was considered by many to be the ideal of the Nazi woman. Upon joining the SS she was sent to Ravensbrück in August 1939. After 1942 she oversaw the training of new guards: in August 1943 she was promoted, and as a member of the command staff between 1943 and 1945 she directed training and assigned duties for over 100 female guards, reputedly training some of the cruelest female guards in the system. She also supervised the bunker where women prisoners were tortured and killed, and she earned the reputation of being sadistic and enjoying witnessing the suffering of others (Adele and Sarti, 2011).

Juana Bormann, likewise, was noted for her brutality (Brown, 2002; Bartrop and Grimm, 2019). Older than most of her peers, she first joined the SS as a civilian employee at Lichtenburg. When Ravensbrück was opened in May 1939 she was transferred there. In March 1942 she was deployed to the main camp at Auschwitz (*Stammlager*), before being sent to its extermination complex at Birkenau. Notorious for beating prisoners, it was said that one of her favorite diversions was unleashing her German shepherd dog (by some accounts, an Irish wolfhound) on the prisoners. Everyone, it was noted, was afraid of her and did their best to avoid her.

One of the most infamous Nazi guards, male or female, was Irma Grese, sometimes called "the Beautiful Beast" (Brown, 1996). By the time she was aged 18 she was accepted to work as a guard at Ravensbrück. She brought to the position both her passion for the Nazi cause and her brutality. In March 1943 she moved to Auschwitz, and by the middle of 1944 she was a senior guard, active in prisoner selections for the gas chambers. She was especially feared by inmates, with survivors later recalling acts of cruelty and bloodshed, such as indiscriminate shootings and beatings. She became a symbol of terror, and the most feared guard in the camp. Her scrupulous personal grooming, tailored clothing, and overuse of perfume were all part of a deliberate act of hostility against the ragged women who were her prisoners.

Maria Mandl was notorious as a top-ranking official at Auschwitz (Fénelon, 1977; Brown, 2002). Austrian by birth, following the *Anschluss* between Austria and Germany in March 1938 she joined the SS and became a guard at Lichtenberg, where she was remembered as standing out from all other guards owing to her brutality and violence. She then worked at Ravensbrück, where newly recruited guards began their training. In October 1942 she was transferred to Auschwitz, working there until November 30, 1944. She was feared and called "the beast" because of her viciousness; one of her protégés was Irma Grese.

Elisabeth Volkenrath trained at Ravensbrück under Dorothea Binz and in 1942 became a supervisor at Auschwitz (Brown, 2002; Bartrop and Grimm, 2019). In 1939 she was called up to work in a munitions factory, but in October 1941 she joined the SS and was transferred to Auschwitz-Birkenau. In August 1942 she began working at the Auschwitz women's camp, and in 1943 while serving as a senior camp guard, she took part in selections and the physical abuse of prisoners. Promoted to senior supervisor in November 1944, she remained at Auschwitz until the final evacuation of the camp complex on January 18, 1945.

When drawing conclusions about women who served as guards in Nazi concentration camps during the Holocaust, we have to ask: how far can the record be considered as representative of the SS female guard corps overall? All those discussed here shared one unifying characteristic: the extraordinary levels of violence they meted out to those under their command. This is something that need not be recapitulated again; the features mentioned here—unfortunately, the tip of a very large iceberg—should suffice. While the guards could not do whatever they liked to prisoners willy-nilly, the range of activities for which they could take action was broad—and the means by which they could do so was limited, in many respects, only by their imagination. That said, perhaps the best summation of what characterized the behavior of the female guards came from a prisoner at Auschwitz, under the direct supervision of Maria Mandl: "Woe to those who forget that everything that resembles a human being is not necessarily a human being" (Fénelon, 1977: 97–98). In a situation where the guards wielded the power of life and death, no alternative could be found for the prisoners but to obey.

By the end of the war, the infamous sisterhood was large, with some 3,500 female guards in all the main concentration camps in Eastern Europe (Dillon, 2015). How they achieved the obedience they demanded was up to each guard herself—but, as we have seen, at least for the tiny sample outlined here, there was never room for kindheartedness or negotiation. Their power was absolute, their fates intertwined; and in that, as we know only too well, lay the reality behind untold desolation and suffering.

PROFESSIONALS: THE MEDICAL PROFESSION

German physicians played a decisive role in the racial programs of the Nazi state. Of all German occupational groups, they had the greatest proportion of members in the Nazi Party (almost 50 percent) and German medicine legitimized the Party's eugenic and racial programs. Such programs were implemented throughout the entire German health care system, with the Nuremberg Laws of 1935 extending state-enforced selection to include race—which was considered a medical issue. Racial inferiority certainly extended to the language of professional discourse that included concepts such as "life unworthy of life" (*lebensunwertes Lebens*).

Under the program known euphemistically as euthanasia, patients medically defined as undesirable were selected for killing. Murder by gas chamber originated in the program, code-named *Aktion T-4*, with the task of turning on the gas assigned to a physician and designated as a medical act.

Universities and research institutes saw concentration camps and the killing programs as opportunities for research in which prisoners became human guinea pigs exploited for deadly medical experimentation. Having been scientifically classified as "life without value," the enslaved human subjects did not qualify for protection against such experiments, and German medical science exploited the Nazi programs to acquire human specimens for institutes of anatomy, pathology, and neuropathology.

Among the activities in which the Nazi doctors engaged, two types stood out. Military experiments, in which the regime sponsored a series of inhumane tests for alleged ideological, military, and medical purposes, included experiments in extreme hypothermia through freezing, high altitude, injections with sea water, sulfanilamide, tuberculosis, poison, and wounds. Racially motivated experiments, on the other hand, were conducted by doctors focusing on achieving certain anthropological, genetic, and racial goals; these included experiments in artificial insemination, sterilization, the study of twins and dwarves, and the study of Jewish skeletons, skin, and skulls.

As with the female guards in the concentration camps, a brief examination of specific medical practitioners can give an idea as to how they contributed to the perpetration of the Holocaust. The following examples will suffice as a representative sample.

Hermann Becker-Freyseng engaged in low-pressure-chamber research to mimic the effects of high altitudes and extremely cold temperatures on the human body, and he forced internees to drink saltwater to measure their bodies' reactions, also injecting saltwater directly into prisoners' bloodstreams to measure the liver's reaction to the saltwater (Lifton, 1986).

Josef Mengele (Ceffrey, 2001), known almost universally as the "Angel of Death," considered that twins held the mysteries behind how Aryan genetic features, such as blonde hair and blue eyes, were passed on; accordingly, he experimented on some 1,500 sets of twins, who, each day, had blood samples drawn from them. He attempted to change eye color by injecting chemicals or giving drops, injected lethal germs, carried out sex change operations, and removed organs and limbs; he also attempted to create conjoined ("Siamese") twins by sewing their backs together and trying to connect blood vessels and organs. Among his other interests were conducting experiments on people with physical abnormalities, such as dwarves and hunchbacks.

Herta Oberheuser was concerned to replicate combat injuries, to understand better how they should be treated in the field or at front-line hospitals (Lifton, 1986). Accordingly, concentration camp inmates were subjected to gunshot wounds infected with dirt and foreign material such as wood, rusty nails, shards of glass, pebbles, dirt, or sawdust; the prisoners also endured deliberately severed muscles and broken bones, and their wounds were then injected with streptococcus, gas gangrene, and tetanus. In addition, Oberheuser conducted experiments involving bone and muscle transplantation, to provide "spare parts" for wounded German soldiers.

Two other doctors engaged in medical experimentation were Eduard Wirths, who undertook gynecological and typhus-related tests and the sterilization of women through the removal of their ovaries (through surgery or radiation); and Karl Gebhardt, who not only broke the arms and legs of women to gauge the body's ability to heal itself, but also introduced infections into deliberately induced wounds in order to test various drugs designed to ward off sepsis and gangrene. In a similar vein, Gebhardt amputated prisoners' limbs and attempted to transplant them onto German soldiers wounded on the Russian front.

In the aftermath of these revelations, there appeared considerable debate over the soundness of the Nazis' lethal experiments on unwilling subjects, and whether data thereby gathered could be used in any way by the scientific community (Proctor, 1988). Such "science" was, of course, completely fraudulent. The responses of the victims never mirrored those for whom the experiments were meant to benefit. Also, the scientific integrity of the experiments was bogus when we consider the Nazi doctors' political aspirations and their enthusiasm for predetermined medical conclusions that "proved" Nazi racial theory. And the fact that the Nazi experiments were rarely, if ever, replicated raises doubts about the data's scientific accuracy.

The Nazi medical experiments were essentially pseudo-science in which the Nazis blurred the distinction between science and sadism. The data was not recorded from scientific hypothesis and research, but rather, was inspired and administered through racial ideologies of mass murder and/or callous torture for its own sake.

PROFESSIONALS: THE LEGAL PROFESSION

Upon attaining office in January 1933, the Nazis began a reorganization of the German judicial system according to their philosophy that the law should not be based on individual rights and equality but rather on the interests of the People's Community (*Volksgemeinschaft*). The supreme aims of the law, henceforth, should be the protection of the German ("Aryan") race, national honor, defense capabilities, and public order. For political opponents and so-called "anti-socials" as well as Jews and "foreigners," special, tougher laws were introduced successively, in order to secure their total obedience to the new regime or to eliminate them (McKale, 1974; Koch, 1997; Maijer, 2003).

After the passage of the Enabling Act on March 23, 1933, the Nazis gradually supplanted the normal justice system with political courts with wide-ranging powers, creating *Sondergerichte* (Special Courts) which operated outside of and free from the previous constitutional court system. Perhaps because they feared that the regular system faced abolition, Germany's judges, lawyers, and legal experts caved in to many of the government's demands. The Nazis did not have to change the court system; the system simply changed for them.

Judges were at the heart of this transformation. They interpreted and enforced Nazi legislation, even their dubious racial and eugenics policies, for the most part without question. They did not question or criticize the Gestapo, which acted beyond the reach of the courts, and acquiesced to Nazi demands for tougher sentences for certain crimes.

A Special Court had three judges, and defense counsel was appointed by the court. Even as heavy-handed as justice was in Nazi Germany, defendants were afforded at least nominal protections under the regular courts' rules and procedures, but these were swept away in the Special Courts which existed outside the ordinary judicial system. There was no possibility of appeal, and verdicts could be carried out at once. The court decided the extent of evidence to consider, and defense attorneys were not permitted to question the proof of the charges.

At almost the same time as the *Sondergericht* system was introduced, and again pursuant to the Enabling Act of 1933, Adolf Hitler ordered the formation of the "People's Court" (*Volksgerichtshof*), which would operate as a special political court outside the existing court system and constitution (McKale, 1974; Miller, 1995). It was established on April 24, 1934, with jurisdiction over a broad range of political offences, and exclusive jurisdiction over such offences as Conspiracy to Commit High Treason, State Treason, Listening to Enemy Radio Broadcasts (from 1939), Criminal Malice, Sedition and Defeatism, and Aiding the Enemy (from mid-1941). "Political crimes" ranged from minor offences—from trading on the black market, work slowdowns, criticizing Hitler or the government, or protesting about work conditions, through to defeatism, espionage and sabotage, and treason against the Third Reich. These offences or crimes were viewed by the court as *Wehrkraftzersetzung* ("incapable of a defense"), and were accordingly punished severely. The court decided the extent of evidence to consider, and defense attorneys could not question the charges.

Almost without exception, cases in the People's Court had predetermined guilty verdicts. There was no presumption of innocence, nor could the defendants adequately represent themselves or consult an attorney. A proceeding before the People's Court would follow an initial indictment in which a state or city prosecutor would forward the names of the accused to the court for charges of a political nature. Defendants were hardly ever allowed to speak to their attorneys beforehand, and when they did the defense lawyer would usually simply answer questions about how the trial would proceed and refrain from any legal advice.

Proceedings in the People's Court began when those accused were led to a prisoner's dock under armed police escort. The presiding judge would read the charges and then call the accused forward for "examination." Although the court had a prosecutor, it was usually the judge who asked the questions.

Defendants were often berated during the examination and never allowed to respond with any sort of lengthy reply. After a barrage of insults and condemnation, the accused would be ordered back to the dock with the order "examination concluded." The defendant was not permitted to choose defense counsel, who had to be a lawyer approved by the chairman of the Senate. Defenders and defendants were often given only a day or even a few hours' notice before the trial to learn of the prosecution allegations. Often the lawyer and the accused did not know each other until the notice of trial, nor could they contact each other before the hearing.

After examination, the defense attorneys would be asked if they had any statements or questions. Defense lawyers were present simply as a formality and hardly any ever rose to speak. The judge would then ask the defendants for a statement during which time more insults and berating comments would be shouted at the accused. The verdict, which was almost always "guilty," would then be announced and the sentence handed down at the same time. In all, an appearance before the People's Court could take as little as 15 minutes.

The death penalty was meted out in numerous cases. There was no possibility of appeal, and verdicts could be carried out immediately. Appointed by Adolf Hitler, judges in the People's Courts were expected to be politically reliable. In some trials, one man alone acted as judge, jury, and court recorder.

The transformation of the German legal code—and, thereby, the profession—took its most dramatic first step when Wilhelm Stuckart, a Nazi Party lawyer, began serving in the Reich Ministry of Interior on March 7, 1935, with responsibility for constitutional law, citizenship, and racial laws (Jasch, 2013). In this role, on September 13, 1935, he, together with Bernhard Lösener and Franz Albrecht Medicus, was given the task of co-writing the antisemitic Law for the Protection of German Blood and German Honor and the Reich Citizenship Law. Together these are better known as the Nuremberg Laws, which enacted the legal basis of Nazi racial policy, removing Jewish participation from mainstream society. The laws deprived Jews of citizenship, prohibited Jewish households from having German maids under the age of 45, prohibited any non-Jewish German from marrying a Jew, and outlawed sexual relations between Jews and Germans (Schleunes, 1970). Drafted in two days, the laws were imposed by the Reichstag on September 15, 1935.

With this as the legal base of Nazi racism, and supported by political regimens imposed by the *Sondergericht* and the *Volksgericht*, the regime saw the complete transformation of what had been the liberal democratic rule of law under the Weimar Republic. These courts did not employ standard legal procedures or principles, such as the presumption of innocence, trial by peers, or the right to cross-examine witnesses.

Roland Freisler exemplified how this was translated into daily practice (Koch, 1997; Stolleis, 1998). A preeminent lawyer and judge, he served as President of the People's Court from August 20, 1942, until his death in Berlin on February 3, 1945.

As President of the court, Freisler was in charge of the show trials used by the Nazis to deal with opponents of the National Socialist regime and political dissent, acting as judge, jury, and sometimes even as prosecutor, handing down the death penalty or life imprisonment in 90 percent of all cases that came before him. While he presided over the First Senate of the People's Court, he was responsible for as many death sentences as all other sessions of the court put together for the entire time it existed.

Freisler contributed to the introduction into German law of racial categories and differential treatment based on race. In addition, he was responsible for the first laws authorizing the execution of juveniles in Germany. He was more extreme even than Adolf Hitler in his adherence to principles of racial purity, arguing for a ban on any sort of mixed-blood intercourse or relationships, no matter how little "foreign blood" might be involved. He represented the Reich Ministry of Justice at the Wannsee Conference in January, 1942, when the plans of the Final Solution, the destruction of European Jewry, were outlined.

Overall, it could be said that the justice system and the legal profession in Nazi Germany made a major contribution to the perpetration of the Holocaust. All actions taken were underwritten by legislation; and when that could not be readily located, judges were required to recognize Adolf Hitler's will as a source of authority that superseded all written law. Only one leading judge in the whole period of the Third Reich, Lothar Kreyssig, took a stand against this, for which he was effectively dismissed. The rest of the profession, almost universally, fell into lock step behind the demands of the Nazi dictatorship.

COLLABORATORS BEYOND NAZI GERMANY

Throughout occupied Europe there were many others who enjoyed the power Nazi authority gave them. Some also exploited the situation for personal gain. Collaborators were to be found in every country, and the Nazis relied upon them to carry out their acts against individuals and communities everywhere (Rings, 1982). They traded, moreover, on local animosities and prejudices. They were happy, for example, for the French to do their dirty work for them; indeed, the Vichy regime hastened to act against its Jews before being required to by the Nazi occupiers. In Croatia, home-grown excesses were so extreme that the Nazis invited their Croat allies to tone down the vehemence of their actions. Romanian brutality against Jews in the occupied Crimea shocked German observers. And in Latvia and Lithuania, the Nazis sought to deflect responsibility for their antisemitic activities by arranging for native collaborators to undertake pogroms on their behalf.

The term "quisling"—a person who collaborates with an enemy occupying force—originated in the person of Vidkun Quisling, Norway's most important collaborator. There were a variety of such people in most of the occupied countries, particularly in France, Belgium, and the Netherlands in Western Europe, and Ukraine and the Baltic States in Eastern Europe. Countries allied with Germany also played their part in the destruction of the Jews.

In many of the countries that might be termed German satellites—whether occupied or allied—a variety of auxiliary forces were brought into the anti-Jewish project, and in some cases their actions were the equal (at least) of Nazi barbarities. The degree to which collaborators supported, facilitated, or were accessories to the Holocaust varied. Some people took part enthusiastically in killing operations, and some enlisted in the Waffen-SS (that is, the military wing of the SS) for active service due to strongly held ideological convictions (Hale, 2011). Indeed, full Waffen-SS divisions—French, Croatian, Danish, Norwegian, Bosnian, Latvian, Dutch, Ukrainian, Belgian, and many others—were created in lands occupied by the Nazis, and then deployed to fight on behalf of Germany. Collectively, these numbered in the hundreds of thousands, adding enormously to the pool of available manpower from whom the Germans could draw. Other collaborators acted from additional motives, which could be financial, careerist, or a fear of retribution if they did not so act. From time to time genuinely held opportunistic motives surfaced; on other occasions, collaborators were prompted to act in especially violent ways owing to unmet socio-pathological needs.

In summary, the Holocaust was visited upon the Jews of Europe by more than Germans alone. Those who carried out the Holocaust were motivated by a longing to destroy a Jewish presence, and all possessed the ability to choose between life and death, between participation and avoidance.

LIVING IN THE GREY ZONE

There were, finally, some Jews who shared, unwillingly, in the killing process—those singled out, for example, as members of the Jewish Councils (*Judenräte*) or Jewish police in ghettos, or *kapos* in the concentration camps. Unlike the perpetrators of various kinds described in this chapter, however, life choices did not exist, and in that sense they could not be viewed as complicit. In most cases they did not have control over their daily activities; they certainly had no control over the time, place, or manner of their death, and were both persecuted by the Nazis and punished by other Jews owing to their involvement. They lived, in a term identified by Italian Holocaust survivor Primo Levi, in the "grey zone" (1989). That zone, as he described it, is the space between absolute good and absolute evil, where moral choices are made for the purpose of survival rather than death, where the desire to live surpasses that to be honorable.

Levi recognized that we should hold back from any condemnation, for example, of the *Sonderkommando* men in the crematoria and gas chambers, where they engaged in the task of doing the physical work of extermination itself, thereby moving the results of Nazi moral choices away from the scrutiny of the Nazis themselves. As Levi wrote,

> one is never in another's place. Each individual is so complex an object that there is no point in trying to foresee his behavior, all the more so in extreme situations; and neither is it possible to foresee one's own behavior.
>
> (1989: 43)

Living in the grey zone presented some Jews with a constant succession of choiceless choices, relentless anguish over actions that would never have been considered viable in the world beyond the Holocaust.

But everywhere, Jews were always vulnerable to discrimination, denunciation, deportation, and, ultimately, extermination. As Rabbi Hugo Gryn, a survivor of Auschwitz, Sachsenhausen, and Mauthausen, was to recall about the Holocaust: "It was the most terrible revelation about the principle of evil. ... We were its victims, and we know who the perpetrators were. And Europe, it seems to me, was a bystander. And this is the essence of the tragedy" (Bloomstein, 1982).

DISCUSSION QUESTIONS

- Were those who perpetrated the Holocaust only Germans?
- Is there any ground for sympathizing with Holocaust perpetrators as casualties of the time and place circumstances in which they found themselves?
- Do you think that recollections from perpetrators written after the World War II are likely to be sincere or accurate? Why/Why not?
- Who had greater responsibility for perpetrating the Holocaust: those who actually did the killing, or those who planned it and gave the orders for it to be carried out?
- Should those caught in the "grey zone"—leaders of the *Judenräte*, Jewish ghetto police, members of the *Sonderkommando* in the extermination camps—also be considered as perpetrators?

JEWS AND OTHER VICTIMS

OVERVIEW

The Nazi regime was responsible for the death of up to 11 million civilians, from all parts of occupied Europe, including around two out of every three Jews living in Europe before the war. All of Europe's Jews were slated for destruction: the sick and the healthy, the aged and the young, the rich and the poor, the religiously observant as well as converts to Christianity.

The destruction was, however, not spread evenly. Despite the Nazi ambition to wipe out all of Europe's Jews, most of those who survived lived in areas not occupied by Germany: Allied states such as Britain and the eastern areas of the Soviet Union, or neutral states like Spain, Turkey, Portugal, Switzerland, and Sweden. Most of Denmark's Jews were rescued *en masse* through being smuggled to Sweden, while the Jews of Bulgaria were saved owing to a refusal on the part of the Bulgarian government to allow their deportation. Tens of thousands of Jews also survived in German-occupied Europe. Some survived in the forests, fighting the Nazis as partisans (though this was extremely hazardous, and many were killed by non-Nazi and non-German antisemites); others lived in hiding, or managed to hold on as prisoners in concentration camps until liberation.

Millions of others, including Roma, German and Austrian homosexuals, political dissidents, Russian prisoners, and Germans with physical or mental disabilities, also lost their lives, though the fundamental difference between their fate and that of the Jews is that the latter were targeted on account of their very birth, a fact embedded into the core of Nazi ideology. Other groups targeted by the Nazis included trade unionists and dissenting clergy. It is testament to the ferocity of the Nazi regime that those imprisoned or in other ways persecuted were often killed, regardless of the reason for their arrest or incarceration.

Given this, it must always be remembered that the Holocaust was a premeditated action by the Nazis to permanently eradicate a Jewish presence in Europe. Others—the disabled, Roma, Poles and other Slavs, Jehovah's Witnesses, homosexuals, dissenting clergy, communists, socialists, "asocials," and political opponents of all sorts—were also persecuted and in many cases murdered in huge numbers; however, it was the campaign against the Jews that was the ideological "ground zero" for Nazi racial ideology. Others besides Jews were murdered, often on a genocidal scale, and should be remembered and acknowledged: but it was only the Jews who were all to be killed as part of a calculated policy of genocide.

THE JEWISH QUESTION

The so-called "Jewish Question" (*Judenfrage*)—that is, the status and place of Jews in Western culture—appeared long before the rise of Adolf Hitler and the Nazis in Germany (Robinson, 2001; Roudinesco, 2014). Where to place the Jews within a majority Christian society was a key issue for many people, over a long period. Prior to France granting the Jews the right to vote as citizens in 1790, the position of Jews was already being discussed in England, resulting in the "Jew Bill" of 1753 (officially passed by Parliament as the Jewish Nationalization Act) and its near-immediate repeal in 1754. Nearly a century before Nazism, German historian Bruno Bauer wrote a book entitled *The Jewish Question*, arguing strenuously that in order for Jews to achieve full emancipation in society and equality within the nation state, they would have to abandon their religious parochialism in favor of a more secular (that is, non-religious) position. Perhaps somewhat ironically, the father of socialism, Karl Marx, himself of Jewish parentage but baptized in infancy by his father, responded with a contribution of his own, *On the Jewish Question*, critiquing Bauer. Marx argued that religion—any religion—is an integral element of modern society, but that individuals tied to it, Jews included, are participants in an oppressive socioeconomic and political system, and that true liberation for the individual must result in a rejection of all forms of religious identification (Maccoby, 2006). Scholars remain divided, however, as to whether Marx furthered the arguments of antisemitism or rejected them.

The year of Adolf Hitler's birth, 1889, saw the rise in Germany of an "Antisemitic German Social Party," a merger of a number of already-acknowledged antisemitic groups committed to displacing the Jews in Germany's social, cultural, and political life. Among its members was Adolf Stoecker, chaplain to Kaiser Wilhelm II, Lutheran pastor, and the founder of the Christian Social Party. Other leading writers and intellectuals in Germany addressing the Jewish Question included Wilhelm Marr (*The Victory of Judaism over Germanism*, 1879); Karl Eugen Düring (*The Parties and the Jewish Question*, 1881); Theodor Fritzsch (*The Handbook of the Jewish Question*, also known as *The Anti-Semitism Catechism*, 1893); Houston Stewart Chamberlain (*The Foundations of the Nineteenth Century*, 1899); and Paul de Lagarde (*German Writings*, 1878–1881).

Hitler himself addressed the Jewish Question in a now-infamous letter to Adolf Gemlich, a German soldier, at the request of Captain Karl Mayr, the head of the Intelligence Section of the *Reichswehr* (Imperial Defense Force). Hitler had become a member of that unit in September 1919. Still in uniform after Germany's defeat, Hitler wrote on September 16, 1919, that

> The danger posed by Jewry for our people today finds its expression in the undeniable aversion of wide sections of our people … Antisemitism as a political movement may not and cannot be defined by emotional impulses, but by recognition of the facts. The facts are these: First, Jewry is absolutely a race and not a religious association … In his effects and consequences he is like a racial tuberculosis of the nations.
>
> (Kershaw, 1999: 125)

Hitler deduced from this that "an antisemitism based on purely emotional grounds will find its ultimate expression in the form of a pogrom" (Kershaw, 1999: 125). On the other hand, a form of antisemitism based on reason "must lead to systematic legal combating and elimination of the privileges of Jews"—in other words, some form of Aliens Law that will distinguish the Jews from "other aliens who live among us." The ultimate objective, however, "must ... be the removal of the Jews in general" (Kershaw, 1999).

THE NATIONAL SOCIALIST PROGRAM

The rise of antisemitism in the nineteenth century, coupled with the trauma of Germany's defeat in the World War I and the craving to apportion blame, led inescapably to the appearance of a number of right wing and antisemitic parties and groups. The 25 Points comprising the National Socialist German Workers' Party (NSDAP) Program were perhaps the clearest expression of such attitudes (Fritzsche, 2008; Orlov, 2008). Composed by Adolf Hitler and the founder of the far-right German Workers' Party, Anton Drexler, the Program was formally unveiled on February 24, 1920, the same day that the German Workers' Party was renamed the National Socialist German Workers' Party.

In the second volume of his book *Mein Kampf*, Adolf Hitler explained that the principles forming the Program had been devised to give "a rough picture" of the movement's aims, which, he wrote, formed "a political creed" intended to recruit new members and reinforce membership for those already in the Party. There had been earlier examples of a similar nature, but here Hitler made it clear that his thoughts would be translated into a plan of action. Although declaring that the Program was designed to be of limited duration, and that party leaders had no intention of establishing any new principles, subsequent events would demonstrate that the 25-Point Program was set in place to stay.

The first principle established the tone for all the others, as a nationalistic statement leaving no room for doubt as to the Nazis' desire to expand Germany's current borders into the future: "We demand the unification of all Germans in the Greater Germany on the basis of the people's right to self-determination" (Bartrop and Grimm, 2019: 315). Given that, Point 2 demanded an overthrow of the post-Great War peace treaties of Versailles (Germany) and St. Germain (Austria), something from which Hitler never retreated and which was to characterize his foreign policy through to 1939.

This opened the way for the points relating to race, Points 4 and 5, respectively. In Point 4, the Program stated that "Only a member of the [German] race can be a citizen. A member of the race can only be one who is of German blood, without consideration of creed. Consequently no Jew can be a member of the race" (Bartrop and Grimm, 2019: 315). As no Jew could be a member of the German race, it figured that, according to Point 5, "Whoever has no citizenship is to be able to live in Germany only as a guest and must be under the authority of legislation for foreigners" (Bartrop and Grimm, 2019: 315). Point 8 spelled out that "further immigration of non-citizens is to be prevented," and that "all non-Germans, who have immigrated to Germany since August 2, 1914, be forced immediately to leave the Reich" (Bartrop and Grimm, 2019: 315).

And so it went on. All areas of public discourse that could revert to Germany were demanded, from the "right to determine matters concerning administration and law," in which "every public office be filled only by citizens" (Point 6); to compulsory nationalization of all trusts (Point 13); to "struggle without consideration" against those "whose activity is injurious to the general interest," such as "Common national criminals, usurers, profiteers and so forth," who would suffer the death penalty for their actions (Point 18); and to a complete overhaul of the "whole national education program" (Point 20) (Bartrop and Grimm, 2019: 315).

Points 24 and 25 summed up where National Socialism was heading: "We demand freedom of religion for all religious denominations within the state so long as they do not endanger its existence or oppose the moral senses of the Germanic race," as a way to combat "the Jewish-materialistic spirit within and around us"; with this, the party demanded a state in which citizens would put "The good of the state before the good of the individual" (Point 24); and, in order to achieve all that the Nazis had set out in their program, "we demand the formation of a strong central power" that would claim "Unlimited authority of the central parliament over the whole Reich and its organizations in general" (Point 25) (Bartrop and Grimm, 2019: 315).

Overall, the 25-Point Program of the Nazi Party showed Hitler's determination to establish a national community (*Volksgemeinschaft*) of mutual interest that asserted racial supremacy for the German people, governed by a strong central authority unhampered by parliamentary procedures rather than one that was divided over differing values or as a result of diverse national backgrounds or religious beliefs.

In subsequent years some members of the party sought to amend the National Socialist Program, but Hitler blocked every suggestion of changing it. It was, for him, sacrosanct, absolute, and permanent. Moreover, it contained much that was a departure from all previous notions of parliamentary democracy, at a time when Weimar Germany was desperately trying to protect the fragile hold on democratic values it was committed to directing.

Hitler would continue to speak out against the Jews, and refine his thinking, writing, and understanding of the Jewish Question. With the Nazi takeover of Germany and Hitler's ascent to the office, the Jewish Question became linked to the NSDAP Program. It was from the foundation of the 25 Points that all Nazi antisemitic measures would be based; while a far cry from what would, by 1941 and 1942, become the Final Solution to the Jewish Question (*Endlösung der Judenfrage*), the evolving plan for the extermination and annihilation of the Jews of Europe had this statement of principles as its initial warrant.

A RANGE OF VICTIMS

The Holocaust is the name most frequently allocated to the Nazi genocide of the Jews, but the number of other people victimized who were not Jewish was staggeringly high. The groups targeted for persecution were numerous, and ranged extremely widely, from people with intellectual disability, physical handicap or incurable disease, to male homosexuals, to Jehovah's Witnesses, to Soviet prisoners of war, to Roma and Sinti, to national groups such as the Poles. The degree of victimization varied considerably from group to group (Berenbaum, 1990).

Starting with the Nuremberg Laws of 1935, and aided by theories of eugenics, Social Darwinism, and post-Enlightenment thinking regarding the progress and scientific perfectibility of human beings, the Nazis turned to the physical sciences for solutions to their question of how to improve society. The Nazi conception saw that all human life constituted an ongoing confrontation for supremacy between competing races of people, a "racial struggle" (*Rassenkampf*). This struggle was both typified by and expressed at its most extreme through an abiding conflict between the Aryan "race" and the Jewish "race"—a conflict, it was argued, that was forced by the Jews for the purpose of subverting the perfect world order in which the Aryans should, by virtue of their superiority, rightly predominate. The *Rassenkampf* was relentless and had to be fought to the death. The victor would see either an ideal future for the world under the unchallenged rule of the Aryans, or a hopeless outlook dominated by the forces of darkness unleashed by the "satanic Jew." The racial struggle, of necessity, had to be genocidal in scope; neither compromise nor mercy would ever be possible if the required victory was to be achieved.

THE T4 EUTHANASIA PROGRAM

"Life unworthy of life" (*Lebensunwertes Leben*) was the Nazi term for those afflicted with hereditary illnesses, including the mentally ill, who were perceived as a political and economic burden to German society and worthy of euthanasia (Aly, Chroust, and Pross, 1994). In July 1933 the Reichstag passed the Law for the Prevention of Offspring with Hereditary Diseases, which, over time, enabled the establishment of centers masquerading as hospitals or research institutions that would compulsorily sterilize those targeted. Over 300,000 people were sterilized under this law. Then, in October 1939, the so-called "*Aktion T4*" program, named for its location at Tiergartenstrasse 4 in Berlin, was initiated (Weindling, 2015). Headed by Reich Chancellery chief Philipp Bouhler and Dr. Karl Brandt, the program's original intention was to kill off disabled infants and young children. Hitler extended this to adults with disabilities as well, so that eventually the program covered the death of men, women, and children considered "unworthy of life."

Aktion T4 was responsible for the death of approximately 250,000 Germans with mental or physical disabilities. At least 5,000 of these were children under the age of 14. Victims were transferred to one of the six killing centers—Brandenburg, Bernburg, Hadamar, Sonnenstein, Grafeneck, and Hartheim—where they were herded into bogus showers and gassed with carbon monoxide. Their bodies were cremated, and their remains sent to their families along with medical documents giving a fictitious cause of death. Very often, the families were sent accounts that had to be paid for the "funeral services" provided by the state.

Although T4 staff worked meticulously to conceal their actions, the rash of mysterious deaths quickly aroused the suspicion of families. Outrage over these extralegal killings saw public protests (especially from the Church), and in August 1941 Hitler officially halted the program. Unofficially, however, the killings continued clandestinely until the end of the war.

Just as the sterilization law was a precursor to euthanasia, so too was *Aktion T4* in relation to the Final Solution. Those who specialized in murdering with lethal injections, and (more importantly) with gas in these killing centers were later recruited into the wartime extermination camps to serve as experts in depersonalized mass murder (see Box 4.1).

BOX 4.1 PORTRAIT OF A SURVIVOR: FRED SPIEGEL

While the story of Anne Frank is well known, that of Fred Spiegel has barely surfaced except among a very limited few. Born in Dinslaken, Germany, in 1932, Spiegel and his sister, Edith, were sent to live with relatives in Holland after *Kristallnacht*, the "Night of Broken Glass"—the anti-Jewish pogrom of November 9–10, 1938, when the Nazis destroyed Jewish homes, shops, and villages in Germany and Austria. Separated from their mother, the Spiegel children were subjected to persecution after the German Army invaded and occupied the Netherlands in May 1940. Fred Spiegel was sent to concentration camps at Vught, Westerbork, and Bergen-Belsen, and was liberated on April 13, 1945. Later, in the fall of 1945, he and his sister were reunited with their mother in England.

The Dutch "transit camp" of Westerbork, located in northeastern Holland just outside of the town of the same name, was established on October 9, 1939, by the Dutch government as a camp to intern illegal refugee Jews from Nazi Germany. Earlier, on December 15, 1938, the government had closed the border to refugees.

When Germany invaded Holland on May 10, 1940, there were some 750 refugees in the camp. The Nazis permitted it to continue operating, and by 1941 its refugee population had grown to 1,100. Of these, most had originally come from Germany.

In early 1942 the camp was enlarged by the German occupation authorities, and on July 1, 1942, the Nazis assumed direct control, turning it into a "transit camp" from which Jews would be deported to Auschwitz. Then, on July 14, 1942, the Nazis made their initial "selection" of who would remain in the camp and who would be sent away. Two days later the first train left with 1,135 deportees on board. By the end of July, nearly 6,000 Dutch Jews had been sent to Auschwitz from Westerbork, where most were gassed. Henceforth, deportation trains left every Tuesday.

Between July 1942 and September 3, 1944 (when the transports stopped), Westerbork was the transit point for about 101,000 Dutch and 5,000 German Jews, sent to their deaths at the Auschwitz and Sobibór. Some 750 Jews also died at Westerbork itself during the German occupation. When Canadian troops liberated the camp on April 12, 1945, about 900 prisoners, most of whom were Dutch Jews, remained in the camp.

As an adult Spiegel provided a testimony which gave a glimpse into the complexity of the Nazi concentration camp system. He showed the categories of transit camp, concentration camp, and extermination camp, which spread throughout Nazi-occupied Europe from the Netherlands to Poland. By 1943 the Nazi concentration camp system in fact functioned in a number of ways: as the means of removing real or potential opposition from German political life; as penal institutions for German criminals; as unofficial prisoner of war camps, generally for Soviet soldiers; as huge reservoirs of slave labor; as centers of agriculture, mining, and industry; as collection and transit points for so-called racial prisoners; and as extermination installations.

Westerbork was a different variety again. As a "transit camp," most prisoners did not remain in the camp for long, but there was also a permanent camp population retained in order to run the enterprise itself. A Jewish council (*Joodse Raad*) was appointed to run the camp and make the deportation selections, and a Jewish police force managed the transfer process and kept order in the camp. Speigel's account discussed the difficulty the Jewish council faced in making decisions, often literally of a life-and-death urgency. The familiarity with which the Jewish policemen confronted their tasks saw the occurrence of a number of anomalies, not the least of which was Spiegel's own salvation from a deportation transport.

In this case, Speigel escaped being put on one of the transports owing to intervention from one of the SS guards supervising the Jewish camp police. When it appeared that he would be put on the train leaving Westerbork, he screamed "I don't want to go onto this train." Alerted to the commotion, the SS guard ordered that Spiegel not be deported. The pure luck and unpredictable behavior of the SS guard rendered this highly unusual occurrence one that could only be put down to a singular case of chance. Spiegel learned later that the train's destination was the death camp at Sobibór, and that all on board were murdered upon arrival.

Westerbork was a camp containing cultural activities, workshops, a school for unaccompanied child refugees, and an orchestra (this not being uncommon in the death camps in the east). Such infrastructure gave a semblance of routine for those living in the camp, providing the SS with a means to compel passive acquiescence from the inmates. This also provided opportunities for the prisoners to engage in acts of corruption to try to buy more time. There was a system in place allowing for deferments and exemptions that would—for a time—delay deportation for certain individuals. Then, once deported themselves, many of the prisoners went quietly with the thought that the camps to which they were going in Poland would be the same or similar to those they were leaving behind in Holland.

Spiegel remained at Westerbork for about eight months. His mother was at that time living in Britain as an *au pair*, a live-in domestic assistant. Through the Red Cross, she was able to send her son letters. Only twenty-five words long (including the address), the existence of these letters proved to be Spiegel's salvation. His "Uncle Max," with him in the camp, decided to try to find a way to safeguard the boy's life by seeing the Nazi commandant of Westerbork, Albert Gemmeker. His aim was to convince Gemmeker that Spiegel and his sister were in fact British citizens rather than Dutch Jews or German refugees, and that, as such, should be kept on the lists of those not to be transported. As proof of their "British" status, Uncle Max took with him the Red Cross letters sent by Spiegel's mother, marked with both Red Cross and British stamps. On the basis of this, Gemmeker considered the children to be foreign nationals, and arranged for them to have deportation deferments from then on.

Though remaining in Westerbork through this ruse, Speigel's uncle, aunt, and cousin were not so fortunate. About six weeks later, Uncle Max's exemption expired, and the family was sent to "the east." After the war, Spiegel learned that they had been deported to Sobibór and gassed on July 2, 1943.

Throughout their experience, Fred Spiegel and his sister were frequently alone and terrified, the more so after their later evacuation from Westerbork and deportation to their final camp at Bergen-Belsen, where they would remain from January 1944 until their liberation in April 1945 (Spiegel, 2004; Bartrop 2014).

EXTENSION OF THE WAR

Such efforts were incorporated into all other killing actions by the Nazis and their allies, thereby transforming beliefs into actions. These took place through the Jews' ghettoization, the onset of the *Einsatzgruppen* on the Eastern Front, and the introduction of death camps throughout Poland. From 1941 onwards, the killing of Jews was conducted systematically in virtually all areas of Nazi-occupied territory, frequently with the active cooperation of local collaborators.

The killing, once commenced, was at its most severe in Eastern Europe (and Hungary from March 1944 onwards). About 5 million Jews were killed in Eastern Europe, including 3 million in occupied Poland and over 1 million in the Soviet Union. In addition, hundreds of thousands of Jews from the Netherlands, France, Belgium, Czechoslovakia, Yugoslavia, and Greece were also murdered, for the most part deported to the Nazi killing centers in Poland. The Jews of Romania were also slaughtered in large numbers between 1941 and 1944, by both Romanians and Germans acting together and separately.

ROMA AND SINTI

The Roma and Sinti are people of mixed ethnic lineage who entered European history as nomads over a long migration period (Lewy, 2001; Kenrick and Puxon, 2009). During the late Middle Ages they began to settle on lands that would eventually comprise Germany, Austria, and Central and Eastern Europe, particularly Hungary, Romania, Bulgaria, Slovakia, Serbia, Poland, and Croatia. Ethnographers theorize that the Roma and Sinti had their origins on the Indian subcontinent. Together, they have often been referred to as "Gypsies," which is viewed by many as highly pejorative.

Roma and Sinti who were in Germany (which had one of the highest concentrations of Roma prior to World War II) endured discrimination and ill treatment many decades before Adolf Hitler came to power in 1933 (Kenrick and Puxon, 2009). Their unique culture, language, dress, and customs made them easy targets. The emergence of Nazi racial ideology during the 1920s subjected them to much harsher treatment. In the Nazi racial conception the Roma were certainly outsiders, and their mixed heritage was deemed a threat to the supposed racial purity of the Aryan race. They were also frequently seen as "habitual criminals," even though there is no evidence to suggest that they were any more inclined towards crime than other Germans.

In June 1933, Hitler's recently installed government enacted the Law for the Prevention of Offspring with Hereditary Defects, which resulted in the forced sterilization of thousands of German Roma. The Law against Dangerous and Habitual Criminals, promulgated in November 1933, brought the arrests and imprisonment in concentration camps of several thousand Roma, who were deemed "antisocial." Additional anti-Roma legislation was passed as the 1930s progressed.

After the *Anschluss* with Austria in March 1938, the Lalleri, a subgroup of the Roma and Sinti who lived in Austria, were similarly oppressed, arrested, and incarcerated. When war came in September 1939, *Reichsführer-SS* Heinrich Himmler became determined to eradicate all Roma because of the belief that they posed a serious security risk.

Nearly all those remaining in Germany were deported to Poland, and in time large numbers were sent to death camps at Chełmno, Treblinka, and Majdanek. Some Roma were also placed in ghettos, moved in as Jews were deported to their deaths. Towards the end of 1942, Himmler decreed that all surviving Roma in Poland and Eastern Europe would be sent to a specific "Gypsy camp" at Auschwitz-Birkenau, where most died by gassing, rampant disease and sickness, or exhaustion from hard labor. In May 1944, with the advance of Soviet troops from the east and the accompanying decision to vacate Auschwitz, the Roma, Sinti, and Lalleri were murdered in vast numbers (Lewy, 2001).

The Nazi effort to exterminate these people resulted in a catastrophe. Although precise numbers of those killed are not available, researchers have estimated that anywhere between 500,000 and 1.5 million Roma, Sinti, and Lalleri died between the early 1930s and the mid-1940s. Perhaps as much as 50 percent of the Roma, Sinti, and Lalleri population throughout all of Europe was wiped out during that period. The *Porrajamos*, a term which means "The Devouring," referring to the period of the 1930s and 1940s, has been largely overshadowed by the much larger Holocaust of the Jewish people. These two horrific developments unfolded at the same time; indeed, many Roma and Sinti prisoners were incarcerated in the same concentration camps that held Jews and other people deemed "undesirable" by the Nazis.

The fundamental difference between the experience of the Jews and the Roma is that for the Nazis the Jews formed a cosmic force that had to be destroyed for the good of all civilization, whereas the Roma were victimized and murdered on grounds of behaving in unsettled ways that did not fit ordered German social norms, of perceived inferior or mixed heredity, or of what the Nazis referred to as "innate criminality."

HOMOSEXUALS

Repressive Nazi measures even extended into the realm of sexuality, and between 1933 and 1944 well over 50,000 male German homosexuals were arrested; 15,000 of them were incarcerated in concentration camps, and 75 percent of these lost their lives (Grau and Schoppman, 1995). In the hate-filled environment of Nazi Germany, male homosexuals were targeted for arrest, incarceration, and sometimes murder. The Nazis were neither the first nor the last to persecute homosexuals, though the severity of persecution during the Nazi era was particularly severe within the context of modern European history.

When Germany became a united empire in 1871, Paragraph 175 of the German constitution criminalized male homosexuality (Plant, 1986). The penalties dispensed to men caught engaging in homosexual acts were limited primarily to incarceration for a short period of time, and in Germany during the interwar period the law was rarely enforced. In fact, a thriving gay and lesbian culture flourished in a number of German cities, particularly Berlin. Most Germans, however, especially those who lived in rural areas, viewed homosexuality and urban culture in general as objectionable and "un-German."

When the Nazis came to power in 1933, they immediately began to enforce anti-homosexuality laws, despite the fact that some Nazis (such as Ernst Röhm, head of the SA) were themselves gay. Lesbian and gay culture in the cities ceased quickly as bars and social clubs were raided, gay men were arrested and thrown into concentration camps, and homosexuals of all socioeconomic classes were harassed. In addition, the Nazis rewrote Paragraph 175. It became a stricter and more punishing law; more behaviors were criminalized, and the severity of punishment increased. Gay men could now be incarcerated for years in concentration camps or prisons, while others were put in institutions for the insane; still others were forcibly sterilized.

The goal of these punishments was either to prevent men from having sex or to educate them to have the "right" kind of sex, that is, heterosexual sex. Nazi racism sought to increase the number of "Aryans," and decrease the number of people of other races. This meant that all German men and women who the Nazis perceived as "Aryan" were encouraged to produce large families. The Nazis targeted gay men in part because they were not fathering children. By incarcerating them, they argued, they could re-educate gay men to be heterosexual, to marry, and to reproduce.

Gay men's experiences under incarceration, however, did not cause them to become heterosexual. In fact, the idea of re-education quickly became transformed into punishment, and gay men suffered terribly. Moreover, they were targeted for violence not only by Nazi camp guards, but also by fellow prisoners, many of whom viewed homosexuality as immoral. Marked with a pink triangle in concentration camps, gay men were beaten, abused, and murdered. Nevertheless, the Nazis did not aim to kill every gay man they incarcerated—that goal was reserved for Jews.

The Nazis were less active in their pursuit of lesbians, whose sexuality they considered only a minor threat to Aryan racial proliferation. Nevertheless, the lesbian community, as well as individual lesbians, experienced significant degrees of repression. Gay (including lesbian) culture went completely underground. Many lesbians hid their identity by marrying men or pretending they were not lesbian. Some were arrested and imprisoned, where they were marked with a black triangle (as "antisocials") and often forced to work in brothels.

JEHOVAH'S WITNESSES

The Jehovah's Witness religious tradition, founded in the United States in the last quarter of the nineteenth century, came into conflict with the Third Reich when Witness beliefs on the nature of the world and its meaning came sharply into conflict with the tenets of National Socialism (Garbe, 2008). Members believe that the world is in its last days and under the rule of Satan. They are witnesses to God (Jehovah), on the stage of history while awaiting the end of the current order, and they are dedicated to spreading knowledge of Jehovah and His plans. Members believe their allegiance as being to God rather than to the political regimes of Satan's world, although they are law abiding and good citizens where their faith allows. They will not swear an oath, vote, bear arms for a civil state, or belong to a political party. In Nazi Germany, this stance led members most dramatically to refuse to enlist or to give the Hitler salute. A bitter conflict with the authorities followed.

The Nazis banned Jehovah's Witness meetings and missionary work, and some Witnesses lost their jobs as civil servants. Others had their children taken away to be brought up in Nazi homes. Of the 20,000 or so Jehovah's Witnesses active in Germany during the Third Reich, many were incarcerated in concentration camps or prisons. Jehovah's Witnesses were among the first Germans to be placed in the camps, where they were often tortured and murdered. While they could obtain release from incarceration upon signing a declaration that they would recognize the authority of the state above their church, many—probably most—refused to do so.

SLAVIC PEOPLES

The term Slavs denotes a variety of ethnicities and nations in Central, Eastern, and Southeastern Europe, speaking languages belonging to the Slavic language group (Dvornik, 1986). All Slavs were seen by the Nazis as inferior within the order of races. In comparison to the Jews, however, they occupied an indeterminate (though lowly) position in the Nazi racial hierarchy. Sometimes referred to as "subhuman" or "Asiatic," they constituted the numerical majority of Nazi victims of annihilation, deportation, and exploitation. While Germany's invasion of Poland, the Soviet Union, and other Slavic lands was probably not motivated by racial considerations alone (for example, the quest for "living space" or an anti-Bolshevik crusade were probably of greater importance that anti-Slavism), the degree of ferocity accompanying these invasions led to the death of millions of Russians, Ukrainians, Poles, and other Slavs.

Soviet prisoners of war, for example, could hope for neither release nor even a modicum of decent treatment under the Nazis. By the end of the war, more than 3.3 million of them had lost their lives. Another 3 million—Poles—died as a result of brutal Nazi occupation policies and a serious attempt from the Nazis to dismantle Poland. The Nazi state sought the subjugation of Slavs as inferiors, and undertook the murder of Slavic elites (such as university faculty, scientists, musicians, writers, and artists) aiming at the destruction of the intellectual and cultural leadership on which statehood and national identity rested.

DISCUSSION QUESTIONS

- Were Jews the only victims of what may be termed the Holocaust? Why/Why not?
- How did Hitler and the Nazis justify their victimization of different groups before and during World War II? Consider especially the contrasting experiences of Jews, political opponents, gays, people with disabilities, and Jehovah's Witnesses.
- "Not all victims were Jews, but all Jews were victims." Discuss.
- In your view, is it accurate to include all victims of the Nazis equally? Consider the motivations, actions, and justifications of the Nazis in framing your answer.
- In view of the intensification of anti-Jewish measures over time, why do you think so many Jews elected to remain in Germany until it was too late to be able to leave?

RESCUE FROM THE THIRD REICH AND THE HOLOCAUST

OVERVIEW

Rescuers were people who rejected Nazi Germany's attempt to disenfranchise, dehumanize, and ultimately destroy the Jews of Europe. They said no in a wide variety of ways, and for a plethora of reasons.

A few individual rescuers, such as Oskar Schindler, Raoul Wallenberg, and André Trocmé, have received widespread public attention. But most remain unknown to the wider public, even though their efforts on behalf of Jews are remarkable and deserving of broader recognition. A few examples will suffice by way of illustration, though thousands of others could be mentioned.

Tina Strobos was a Dutch medical student who, with her mother, helped save more than a hundred Jews from the Nazis during World War II by giving them refuge on the upper floor of her Amsterdam home—just a few blocks away from another safe house in the same neighborhood, where Anne Frank and her family were being shielded by Miep Gies and others (Gies, 1987; Muller, 1998).

Ho Feng-Shan was the Chinese consul to Vienna, and one of the first diplomats to save Jews by providing them with visas to escape Nazi Germany. Between 1938 and 1940 he was responsible for saving thousands of Jews in Nazi-occupied Austria. For continuing to issue visas despite a direct order for him not to do so, a black mark, or "demerit," was entered into his personnel file in 1939. He continued issuing visas, however, until recalled to China in May 1940. It is not known how many entries he actually authorized prior to then, but there is solid room for speculation that many, probably numbering in the thousands, were issued (Feng-Shan, 2010; Paldiel, 2007a).

María Errázuriz was a Chilean woman who worked with the French Resistance during the Nazi occupation of France in World War II, saving Jewish children at considerable risk to her own life. Captured and tortured, she never broke when demands were made to reveal where she had hidden the children in her care (Bartrop, 2016).

William L. Shirer was an American journalist, war correspondent, and historian, perhaps best known for his book *The Rise and Fall of the Third Reich*. Wherever possible, he took a stand against the Nazis through his reportage, but there was only so much on which he could report; his outgoing dispatches were watched carefully by the Nazis as a condition of his credentials being respected, or he would have been expelled. Despite this, he and his Austrian-born wife Tess sheltered Jews in their home as a refuge for those who had gone into hiding. Occasionally the Shirers would find themselves harboring a Jewish man who had just been released from a jail or concentration camp. In such circumstances, their guest would often have been badly beaten or mistreated, and they would care for him until he had recovered sufficiently to be able to return to his family in something resembling a passable condition (Wick, 2011; Cutherbertson, 2015).

Well over 26,000 rescuers have been recognized by Yad Vashem, Israel's Holocaust Memorial Authority situated in Jerusalem (as described below), honoring non-Jews who risked their own lives, and often those of their families, to save Jews during the Holocaust, as "Righteous among the Nations." This is generally acknowledged as the highest form of recognition that can be bestowed upon non-Jews who saved Jews. The honorific does not extend to the large number of Jews who worked to rescue other Jews during the Holocaust, and there were many who managed to find ways to save their fellow Jews; among these were Wilhelm Bachner, Moussa Abadi, Marianne Cohn, Mila Racine, Aron Grünhut, Rabbi Regina Jonas, and Walter Süskind (Bartrop, 2016; Paldiel, 2017).

Saving lives during the Holocaust was sometimes next to impossible. It was a time when living space, food, sanitation facilities, and medicine were at a premium. Given the enormous risks involved in undertaking rescue efforts, it is remarkable that any of these initiatives took place at all. When we ask, therefore, why there were so few such examples during the Holocaust, the question could more readily be, in view of everything people faced, how come there were so many?

Rescuers existed in all countries under Nazi occupation. They came from all walks of life, belonged to every nationality, confessed to every religious belief, and belonged to all age groups and social classes. They comprised both men and women; some were educated, others not.

During the Holocaust rescuing Jews was very far from being a soft option, and all too frequently choosing to become a rescuer was fraught with emotional, moral, and physical dilemmas. To stand out from the crowd, to refuse to acquiesce, to not compromise one's own values in order to guarantee personal safety at the expense of that of others—these were grueling issues for people to confront during this most extreme time. Human behavior during the Holocaust, it might be said, was the paradigmatic example of all the best—and the worst—that human civilization carries within it, and those who rescued Jews were among the finest examples of human beings acting under conditions of extreme stress on behalf of others.

RIGHTEOUS AMONG THE NATIONS

By an Act of Israel's Knesset (parliament) in 1953, non-Jews who risked their own lives, and often those of their own families, to aid or rescue Jews, have been recognized as "Righteous among the Nations." The term is taken from the Talmud ("the righteous of all nations have a share in the world to come," Talmud Bavli Tractate Sanhedrin 105a). Although the term had been used by rabbis in a religious sense as early as the tenth century CE to designate those Christians who, by their merit, are as eligible as any member of the House of Israel to enter Heaven, it has come more readily to mean non-Jews who risked their lives to save Jews during the Holocaust.

Acts of rescue included sheltering Jews seeking to avoid capture by the Nazis, supplying false documents, providing food, clothing, and shelter, and guiding Jews to places of safety, among many other rescue efforts. Those who are recognized as Righteous have been honored at Yad Vashem, Israel's Holocaust memorial authority in Jerusalem, since the early 1960s. After an exhaustive investigation process, if a person's actions during the Holocaust are deemed to be sufficiently worthy of elevation to the status of Righteous, either the honoree or his or her heirs are invited to Jerusalem to receive the award of a plaque from Yad Vashem and to have the name added to those on the Wall of Honor in the Garden of the Righteous in permanent commemoration of the act for which they are being acknowledged. In earlier times the honoree was entitled to plant a carob tree in the garden, but this had to be discontinued owing to a lack of space (Gilbert, 2002; Paldiel, 2007b). Under Israeli law, recognition of Righteous status enables Yad Vashem to confer honorary Israeli citizenship upon the honoree, in recognition of their actions.

Identification and recognition of such people has been the responsibility since 1963 of a commission headed by a justice of Israel's Supreme Court, whose duty is to investigate cases brought before it and then, when appropriate, grant the award. A very tight set of criteria have been established in order to enable the commission to do its work. These include the following: only a Jewish party can put a nomination forward; helping a family member, or assisting a Jew to convert to Christianity, is not a criterion for recognition; assistance has to be sustained and/or substantial; and assistance has to be given without any financial gain expected in return (although covering normal expenses such as rent or food is acceptable).

Nechama Tec, a Holocaust survivor and professor of sociology, has suggested six common characteristics of the Righteous: individuality or separateness from their social environment; independence or self-reliance; a commitment to helping the needy; a modest self-appraisal of their extraordinary actions; unplanned initial engagement in Jewish rescue; and universalistic perceptions of Jews as human beings in dire need of assistance. That said, it must be emphasized that non-Jewish rescuers during the Holocaust acted from a wide variety of motives, while sharing in common the distinction that they all saved Jews from the fate intended by the Nazis (Tec, 1986).

Some names of those recognized as Righteous stand out in public memory, even today. Raoul Wallenberg and Oskar Schindler have been mentioned. To these could be added the Swiss Vice-Consul to Budapest, Carl Lutz, who, similarly to Wallenberg, used his influence to guarantee the lives of over 62,000 Jews in Hungary; an Italian citizen, Giorgio Perlasca, who posed as a Spanish diplomat in order to save over 5,000 Jews, again in Budapest; the Japanese Consul-General in Kaunas (Kovno), Lithuania, Chuine "Sempo" Sugihara; Miep Gies, who aided the family of Anne Frank; and the inhabitants of the French village of Le Chambon-sur-Lignon under its Huguenot pastor, André Trocmé (Bartrop, 2016).

Since 1962 Yad Vashem has recognized those deemed to be Righteous from forty-four different countries and nationalities. There are Christians from all denominations and churches; Muslims as well as agnostics; and men and women of all ages. The number of Righteous is updated at the beginning of each year and released later: as of January 2018, for example, the award of Righteous status had been made to some 26,973 people, literally from all over the world. Some 6,863 were from Poland, 5,669 from the Netherlands, 4,056 from France, 2,619 from Ukraine, and 1,742 from Belgium. Others ranged from several hundred to (in the case of a number of countries) one individual (www.yadvashem.org/righteous/statistics.html) (see Box 5.1).

BOX 5.1 PORTRAIT OF A RESCUER: JOHANNES BOGAARD

Johannes Bogaard was a Dutch farmer who rescued 300 Jews during the Holocaust. Coming from a devout Christian family and taught by his father to respect the Jews as the people of the Bible, Bogaard—with only a poor formal education—nonetheless felt a responsibility towards helping Jews fleeing from the Nazis.

Born in 1881 in the small farming community of Nieuw Vennep, not far from Amsterdam, Johannes Bogaard, known as Hannes, was raised in a Calvinist family where the Jews were known as God's "chosen people." In view of that, he had little difficulty in recognizing his duty when the Nazis began deporting Jews from the Netherlands in July 1942.

Unhesitatingly, Bogaard and his family decided to try to find a way to help Jews escape deportation. He would do this by hiding Jews on his farm, and prevailing upon his relatives and neighbors to do likewise.

Before the war, Bogaard had had only a very limited experience of Jews. He was acquainted with only one Jewish family, the Mogendorffs, who lived in Amsterdam. Knowing them to be in danger, he took a train—for the first time in his life—and visited them in Amsterdam. He offered them a refuge, initiating a series of actions that saw him contact other Jews to whom he made the same offer. He began making the trip to Amsterdam more frequently, once or twice a week, and shuttled the Jews back to Nieuw Vennep. He also visited Rotterdam and other cities, and repeated the process. So keen was he to collect as many people as possible that at one time he was harboring as many as a hundred Jews.

The help he provided extended beyond simply hiding Jews. He also organized ration cards, money, and false identity papers, and arranged for most of the Jews to be moved to safer locations afterwards. Two of Bogaard's brothers, Antheunius and Willem, were responsible for ensuring a supply of rye, wheat, and other food to the refugees.

The rescue network Bogaard created operated for a year and a half, quite independent of any institutional support from the organized Dutch resistance movement. This came to an end in November 1942, however, when the farm was raided by Dutch Nazis, and eleven Jews were found and deported. Over the next few months the farm was raided twice more, with other Jews captured.

What the raids pointed to was the extent to which the rescuing of Jews was a Bogaard family affair. The hidden Jews were to a large degree cared for by Bogaard's daughter, Metje, and his sister, Aagje. Most of the Jews were concealed at the farm of Hannes Bogaard's father, the 77-year-old Johannes "Grandpa" Bogaard, Sr.

On October 6, 1943, the farm was again raided, with thirty-four people found and deported. During the raid,

Willem Bogaard managed to save a large group of Jewish children, who were hidden elsewhere by Antheunius once the SS men had left. All of them save one subsequently survived the war. Bogaard's daughter Metje managed to save another group during the raid. However, the Jews who were hidden with another of Bogaard's brothers, Pieter, were caught.

Grandpa Bogaard was arrested and detained for ten weeks at the Amstelveenseweg prison in south Amsterdam. He was offered his freedom by the Gestapo only if he undertook not to repeat his offence, but this he refused to do. It would cost him his life; sent to Sachsenhausen, he was murdered there on February 15, 1945. Pieter Bogaard died at his home on September 15, 1944, after months of imprisonment at Holland's Vught concentration camp.

After this, Hannes Bogaard went into hiding, but this did not see an end to the family's efforts on behalf of Jews. His wife Klaasje continued the work of her husband, hiding four Jews on the farm. She was, however, denounced, forcing her to flee and join Johannes. The Jews she was shielding were killed, along with other members of her family.

Although Hannes and Klaasje Bogaard survived the war, their family structure had been devastated. On the positive side of the ledger, however, estimates placed the lives of some 300 Jews directly at their feet. The number of their descendants by now can be measured in the thousands.

Johannes Bogaard died on May 31, 1963, at the age of 83. On October 22, 1963, Yad Vashem recognized him as one of the Righteous among the Nations for his selfless actions in saving the lives of Jews during the Holocaust. Several years later, on August 15, 1974, Antheunius and Willem Bogaard were similarly recognized. The example set by this family, who refused to acquiesce to the Nazi horror, is both inspirational and an outstanding witness to their religious faith during the darkest of times (Paldiel, 1993; Bartrop, 2016).

TWO OF THE RIGHTEOUS

Margit Slachta was a Hungarian pioneer in social service and a leading political figure in interwar Hungary. During the Holocaust, members of the religious order she founded, the Sisters of Social Service, worked to protect their Jewish neighbors while at the same time continuing their commitment to social justice (Paldiel, 1993; Reeves, 2011).

Born in Kassa, Hungary on September 18, 1884, she lived with her parents in the United States when she was a child but returned to Hungary before the turn of the century. Upon her return, she taught French and German at a Catholic school in Budapest. In 1908 she joined a religious community, the Society of the Social Mission. She became an activist for social causes, establishing the Union of Catholic Women, an organization to promote the female franchise in Hungary. As early as 1919 she organized the Catholic Women's Party, and in 1920 became the first woman to be elected to the Hungarian Parliament (for a term lasting two years), where she campaigned on behalf of women, children, families, and the safeguarding of workers' rights.

On May 12, 1923, Margit Slachta founded a new order, the Sisters of Social Service, whose members were dedicated to carrying out their commitment to care for those in need and combat the suffering around them. Over time, the Sisters became well known throughout Hungary for nursing, midwifery, and taking care of orphans.

As an outspoken woman, committed Christian, and promoter of socially advanced causes, she defied the spirit of the age. When Hungary began to introduce measures discriminating against Jews, it was inevitable that Mother Margit (as she now was) would rebel against such developments. With the first anti-Jewish laws appearing in Hungary in 1938, she began publishing articles opposing official antisemitism in her newspaper, *Voice of the Spirit*. In 1943 the paper was suppressed, but Mother Margit continued to publish it underground. Sisters were instructed to familiarize themselves on Jewish matters, and prepare accordingly.

Mother Margit's political activities increased as World War II was unleashed, with the German invasion of Poland in September 1939 leading to waves of Jewish refugees seeking sanctuary. In

1940 Hungary joined the Axis Powers, and that fall, before the Nazis insisted on it, deportations of Jews began in certain regions of the country. Mother Margit responded immediately by agitating for these actions to be stopped, and in one region, at least, the deportations ceased as a result of her actions.

Beyond this, she also provided shelter, and protested against forced labor and antisemitic laws. In 1943, she even went to Rome to try to persuade the Vatican to step in and intervene to stop the persecution of Jews in Slovakia.

Mother Margit instructed her Sisters that they had a bounden duty to protect the Jews, even at the risk of their own lives. She considered it a theological matter, in view of the fact that the Jews were God's people and the people from among whom Jesus was born and raised.

Between July 15 and August 12, 1941, any Jews living in Hungary who could not prove legal residency since 1850 were deported to southern Poland, there to await their fate at the hands of the Germans. It is estimated that this numbered about 20,000 people. Upon learning this, Mother Margit demanded that the process be stopped, protesting directly to Magdolna Purgly, the wife of Hungary's Regent, Miklós Horthy.

When the Nazis occupied Hungary in March 1944, bringing the full weight of the Holocaust with them, the Sisters of Social Service began to arrange baptisms of convenience in the hope that by doing so they would be able to spare Jews from deportation. As things got worse, the Sisters focused completely on helping the Jews. Giving of themselves selflessly, they hid at least 1,000 Jews, and provided food and safe houses whenever they could for fugitives.

Following Mother Margit's lead, one of the Sisters, Sára Salkaházi, took the admonition to offer her life for the Jews literally. She personally saved about a hundred Jews, and as the persecution intensified during 1944, she redoubled her efforts to save as many as she could. Eventually, she was caught by Hungarian Arrow Cross soldiers and murdered on the banks of the Danube on December 27, 1944. Her body was never recovered.

In a singular act of defiance once the Nazis had invaded, Mother Margit began to live in the order's Mother House, located on Budapest's Thököly Street. This acted as a place of refuge for Jews, but its location was both ironic and a challenge, as it was situated right opposite the 14th District Arrow Cross party headquarters. At one point, gangs invaded the House and carried out a brutal hunt for Jews, attacking Mother Margit as well as several of the Sisters. On this occasion she only narrowly avoided execution.

With the end of the war, Mother Margit Slachta became a member of the Hungarian Parliament during the democratic period prior to the communist takeover. At the end of 1948 she fled Hungary for the West, arriving in the United States on June 22, 1949. On January 6, 1974, she died, aged 89, in Buffalo, New York. In acknowledgement for her work in hiding, supplying basic goods, and providing false evidence when in the process of saving Jewish lives during the Holocaust, she was recognized by Yad Vashem on February 18, 1969, as one of the Righteous among the Nations.

Heinz Drossel, born in 1916, finished his law degree just before war broke out in 1939, but was denied entry to the German legal profession owing to his refusal to join the Nazi Party. In November 1939 he was drafted into the German Army, serving during the Battle of France in 1940 (Stegelmann, 2014).

In the summer of 1941 Drossel's resistance to Nazism began when he was ordered to execute a Russian officer. He refused, leading him instead into the forest and sending him back towards Soviet lines. Then, when his unit captured another officer, Drossel defied his orders to take him back to headquarters—where he knew the prisoner would be shot—and turned him loose instead, saying "I am no killer. I am a human being."

On leave in Berlin in 1942, Drossel encountered a distressed young Jewish woman, Marianne Hirschfeld, about to leap from a bridge. He took her to his family's empty apartment, provided her with money for sustenance and so she could find a safe place to stay before he returned to his unit, and then left. His concern was with people's welfare, not the rules that could get him into trouble.

In early 1945 Drossel continued helping Jews. In Senzig, Brandenburg, where his parents had sought safety from Allied bombing raids, he was visiting while again on leave. Knowing that he was an officer, a local Nazi supporter denounced to him a number of Jews who had been living in the community on forged papers. The result saw Drossel's immediate assistance offered to Jack and Lucie Hass, their daughter Margot, and her friend (and later husband), Ernst Fontheim. Without hesitation, he took Jack Hass and Ernst Fontheim back to the empty apartment in Berlin, while he found a safe house for Lucie Haas and Margot. Again, by helping Jews he placed himself at considerable risk, but their lives were saved.

In the spring of 1945 Drossel was captured by advancing Soviet troops, but by a stroke of good fortune he was released and able to return home by the end of the year. Then, in a freak encounter on the streets of Berlin, he met Marianne Hirschfeld, the Jewish woman he had saved in 1942. After he had hidden her in his parents' apartment, she had survived in hiding, and was practically the only member of her family to have escaped the Holocaust. A relationship developed; in 1946 they married and began to raise a family.

Drossel then sought to rekindle his legal career, cut short by his refusal to join the Nazi Party in 1939. He was appalled by what he saw in the legal profession, as many former Nazis were given leave to continue their careers. Over time he progressed, and eventually became a successful lawyer and then a judge. In 1981 he retired, respected by all those around him.

Though he never spoke about his resistance to the Nazis during the war, those whom he had helped had not forgotten him. In 2000 he was honored by Yad Vashem as one of the Righteous among the Nations for his efforts in helping to save Jewish lives. In April 2008 he died in Simonswald, Baden-Württemberg, aged 92.

THE EVIAN CONFERENCE

The role of the international community is highly complex and detailed and cannot be summarized easily. Before 1939 the main responses to Nazi persecution within Germany and Austria ranged between avowed horror on the one hand, and indifference on the other. Rarely was any serious action taken against Germany, though in the early days several leading Nazis were concerned that the regime's anti-Jewish measures might have a negative impact on the economy should other countries respond to defend the Jews' human rights. Such action, however, never materialized.

The major international response during the 1930s took the form of restrictive refugee immigration policies. Just as the Nazis were keen for Jews to leave Germany, most countries outside sought to deny them entry. While all countries developed their own responses individually—with a mixture of cautious acceptance and outright rejection—everything seemed to come to a head when an international conference on refugees took place in the summer of 1938 (Bartrop, 2018).

This conference, which convened in the resort town of Evian, France, between July 6–15, 1938, met at the invitation of United States President Franklin Delano Roosevelt with the intention of discussing, in depth, the nature of the immigration policies of the invited nations, and, in accordance with those, what the options were for accepting refugees from Germany. The countries attending were not expected in any way to depart from their existing immigration regulations. When the meeting's final recommendations were made no definite action on behalf of the refugees was proposed—only that the deliberations should continue, and a subsequent meeting should take place in London.

The Evian Conference became a joint global effort which sought, effectively, to do nothing, and it was successful in achieving its key aim, namely, to enable an exchange of information among the states attending, and nothing more. Roosevelt's initiative in calling the meeting was not intended to compromise the existing policy of any country. Sent out to a number of countries around the world, the U.S. invitation revealed the following features: no particular ethnic, political, or religious group should be identified with the refugee problem or the calling of the conference; nothing should be done to interfere with the operations of existing relief organizations; all assistance for refugee work should be drawn from purely voluntary sources; and no nation should be required to amend its current immigration laws to accommodate the refugees.

Moreover, the agenda, once set, saw that the committee would meet to consider

- what steps could be taken to facilitate the settlement "of political refugees from Germany (including Austria)";

- what steps could be taken to assist the most urgent cases "within the existing immigration laws and regulations of the receiving countries";
- how to establish "a system of documentation, acceptable to the participating States, for those refugees who are unable to obtain requisite documents from other sources";
- the establishment of a more permanent body that would continue the work begun at this meeting;
- and the preparation of a resolution that would make recommendations with regard to the other agenda items (Bartrop, 2018).

Once convened, the Conference would be dominated by three men: Myron Taylor from the United States, Edward Turnour and Lord Winterton from Britain, and Henry Bérenger from France. When they made their various presentations, each stated essentially that they were far from prepared to do anything that would expand Jewish refugee immigration to their respective countries. This then gave a lead to all the other countries, as they, too, lined up to make their presentations. Grouping them into blocs, we can see a number of themes for each.

The European states essentially showed hesitation over the possibility of supplanting or replicating the League of Nations High Commission on Refugees, and argued that they were only prepared to accept refugees for temporary asylum in a short-term transit capacity. The Latin American states (the largest contingent at Evian) were keen to align with Roosevelt's call to link arms in the effort to ease refugee distress and find a way to accommodate them, and noted that the refugee crisis was a humanitarian disaster. At the same time, they asserted that refugees would be admitted only in accordance with existing laws, that only those engaged in farming would be admitted as immigrants, and that no special financial arrangements would be made to assist refugee entry. The British Dominions, similarly, were unhelpful in their attitude, informing delegates that they had neither an interest in—nor a serious desire to help the resolution of—the refugee problem. Canada only wanted farmers; New Zealand did not want foreigners; Ireland did not see itself as an immigrant-receiving country; and the Australian delegate declared that "as we have no real racial problems, we are not desirous of importing one by encouraging any scheme of large-scale foreign migration" (Bartrop, 2018). South Africa declined to attend the Conference altogether.

There were a number of areas in which the Evian Conference, when measured against the standards of 1938, was clearly deficient. Even if the Holocaust could not have been foreseen, the possibility of war nonetheless could be, but at Evian there was no discussion of what would happen to the Jews of Eastern Europe should Germany embark on a war of conquest and thereby increase the number of Jews under Nazi rule. The Conference never managed to resolve its points of crossover with the League of Nations High Commission and other refugee bodies, and it failed to suggest any sort of financial arrangements for the refugees. Nor, shamefully, did the delegates even condemn the Nazi antisemitic persecution that led to the refugee crisis in the first place, with the issue not even raised. These were all within the Conference's remit as targets that could have been met, but none of them were.

That said, it is important to point out that no-one could have foreseen the Holocaust that was to come, and thus the sense of humanitarian urgency was less pressing than it would become in later years. Every country in the world was formulating and administering an immigration or refugee policy—not a rescue-from-the-Holocaust policy.

One final, key question needs to be asked: could the Evian Conference have made a difference to the events that were to follow? The best answer is only: perhaps. Evian *could* have acted as an occasion for caring administrations to voluntarily make some kind of announcement that they would agree to an increase in their refugee or immigration intakes. However, questions of *realpolitik*, racial and population preferences, antisemitism, economic priorities, and other factors led to a collective rejection of any liberalization in favor of Nazi Germany's unwanted Jews. No other outcome was ever likely at this meeting, and the hopes of many were consequently both misplaced and unrealizable.

The immediate results of the Conference amounted to nothing of any lasting worth for the refugees, which was exactly what was anticipated. The assembled countries used the opportunity presented in order to look good, but the refugees got nothing from it. However, Adolf Hitler, who, uninvited, had sent an observer to the Conference, realized that the nations attending would not do anything tangible to assist the Jews—and so, as a result, their fate would be in Germany's hands (see Box 5.2).

BOX 5.2 BRITISH DIPLOMATS AND THE *KRISTALLNACHT*

Reactions among British diplomats in Germany to the events of the *Kristallnacht* pogrom in November 1938 were immediate. Arguably the first official comment to arrive at the British Foreign Office came in during the morning of Thursday November 10, 1938. With the Ambassador to Berlin, Sir Nevile Henderson, in London being treated for the cancer that eventually killed him, the embassy was left in the hands of the *Chargé d'Affaires*, Sir George Ogilvie-Forbes. On November 10 he sent a telegram to the Foreign Secretary, Viscount Halifax, reporting that anti-Jewish rioting on an unprecedented scale had broken out late the night before in Berlin, with similar reports coming in from across Germany.

Ogilvie-Forbes then wrote, on November 14, that many Jews were wandering aimlessly in the streets and parks, afraid to return to their homes. He could not contain his outrage at what he was witnessing, informing the Foreign Office that in his view up to half-a-million Jews were now in danger of their lives.

The lead given by Ogilvie-Forbes was picked up by other British diplomats stationed in Germany. Robert Smallbones was the British Consul-General in Frankfurt am Main, where he had been working since 1932. He was in London when the *Kristallnacht* pogrom took place, and immediately sought out leading members of the Home Office to see what could be done to alleviate distress for the Jews in Frankfurt affected by the violence. He was told by a senior Home Office bureaucrat that nothing could be done: "What can we do? We cannot let them come in and cause unemployment amongst our own people." He then laid a challenge down to Smallbones: "Do you have an idea?" He did, realizing that the first thing needed was to get the men released from the camps into which they had been thrown after November 9–10. Evidence that a British visa had been authorized could secure a man's release from a concentration camp, but Jewish women and children would not be permitted to emigrate from Nazi Germany without the male breadwinner of the family present.

Smallbones contacted the Home Secretary, Sir Samuel Hoare, and presented a plan that would allow for a limited two-year transit visa for German Jews to come to the United Kingdom while awaiting an entry visa from a third country. While in Britain, they would not be allowed to seek work, but they would, nonetheless, be safe. Without seeing a need for this to be discussed in parliament, Hoare accepted the proposal. As a result of what became known as the "Smallbones System," by October 1939 some 48,000 Jews from Germany had arrived in Britain, their lives saved for the time being.

Smallbones received enormous help from his Vice-Consul, Arthur Dowden, who worked to ensure that the British visas were actually delivered to the threatened Jewish families. In addition, given that Jews were not permitted to buy food for nine days after the pogrom, he provided practical help in the form of deliveries of food. Dowden was remembered as driving through the streets, with food in his car, distributing food to those in want. With Smallbones away in London, Dowden took it upon himself to open up the Consulate, where hundreds of Jews spent the night until the threat of arrest was dispelled.

British diplomats in other locations were just as active in their response. John Carvell, Consul-General in Munich, issued certificates permitting 300 Jewish men to be released from Dachau to travel to British Mandate Palestine; his Vice-Consul, Frank Fulham, was particularly interested in saving children, while Donald St. Clair Gainer, who had formerly been in Munich and was now Consul-General in Vienna, reported to the Foreign Office faithfully and with

> horror the destruction of synagogues in Salzburg and Linz, as well as in various locations in Vienna.
>
> We can only speculate as to what might have been the British diplomatic response to the *Kristallnacht* had the Ambassador, Sir Nevile Henderson—an arch appeaser—been present in November 1938, but the reality was that his deputy in Berlin and his consuls outside the capital met and confronted the challenge head-on and in a compassionate manner that saved tens of thousands of Jewish lives (Gilbert, 2008).

THE *KINDERTRANSPORT*

Almost as an answer to the Evian Conference, some individuals decided to take matters into their own hands, realizing that if every Jew in Germany could not be saved then an effort should at least be made on behalf of the children. The response was the *Kindertransport*, organized in the immediate aftermath of the *Kristallnacht* pogrom of November 9–10, 1938 (Samuels, 2010; Byers, 2011). With this, the British government approved a measure to allow the entry of Jewish refugees ranging in age from infants to 17, on the proviso that they had a place to stay and landing money of £50 to enable them to eventually return home. On December 2, 1938, the first group of Jewish children arrived in Britain.

Much of the preliminary work was done by Jewish relief organizations, who planned to rescue the children in what was nicknamed the "children's transport" (*Kindertransport*) program. Ultimately, the initiative would bring some 10,000 unaccompanied children to safety in Britain prior to the outbreak of war in September 1939. The formal name of the rescue effort was the Refugee Children Movement. For the most part, Jewish children from Germany, Austria, Czechoslovakia, and Poland were relocated between December 1938 and September 1939. The rescued children were resettled in hostels, foster homes, and sometimes on farms.

On November 15, 1938, in the immediate aftermath of *Kristallnacht*, Jewish leaders in Britain appealed directly to Prime

Minister Neville Chamberlain for help in rescuing Jewish children. Specifically, they asked that immigration requirements be altered so that unaccompanied Jewish children might be allowed into the country on a temporary basis. In short order, the British Parliament took up the issue and agreed to the request, deciding not to set a limit on the number of children to be admitted. Various Jewish relief agencies swung into action, as did the World Jewish Relief Fund, which worked with British officials in identifying children to be moved and planning for their transport and resettlement.

Once word was received of the British offer, Jewish community organizations in Germany and Austria planned the best ways to send the children to safety. Parents would send letters through bodies such as the Hebrew Immigration Aid Society (HIAS) to sponsors in Britain; some of these sponsors were Jewish, many were not.

Within days of the public announcement of the *Kindertransport* program, some 500 British households offered to take in a child (and, sometimes, more than one). Children were sent by train to the Netherlands or Belgium, and then by boat to Harwich in southeast England, where they were oriented and then handed over to waiting families. The children left their homes without valuables, a maximum of ten marks (the figure set by German authorities for all émigrés), and one small suitcase. None were accompanied by their parents; a few were babies carried by other children. Most were marked with a name tag on their clothes for the purpose of identification.

The first *Kindertransport* left Berlin on December 1, 1938, bringing 196 children from a Jewish orphanage burned down by the Nazis during the night of the pogrom on November 9. It arrived in Harwich the following day.

Most transports left by train from Vienna, Berlin, Prague, and other major cities. Hundreds of children who did not go straight to Britain remained in Belgium and Holland, safe for the time being. On one occasion, a Dutch social worker, Geertruida Wijsmuller-Meijer, went to Vienna to see Adolf Eichmann in person, demanding that he permit children to leave for the United Kingdom immediately. After suffering many indignities at the hands of the Gestapo, she was granted permission to take 600 children out of Vienna, and the first *Kindertransport* from Austria was able to proceed.

In England a number of hostels were administered by members of the Zionist Habonim youth movement in order to house the children. Many others spent time with English families in cities or on farms in the countryside.

Later, after the Germans invaded Czechoslovakia, the program was expanded to include Czech children, in an initiative that lay directly at the feet of a British Jew acting in a private capacity, Nicholas (later Sir Nicholas) Winton (Emanuel and Gissing, 2011). Several groups also came from Poland, especially during the summer of 1939.

The *Kindertransport* program effectively ended in September 1939, when Germany attacked Poland, though one last transport for Britain left from the Dutch port of Ijmuiden on May 14, 1940, one day before Holland surrendered. The eighty children on board had been brought by earlier transports to what was expected to be a safe haven in the Netherlands.

CENTRAL OFFICE FOR JEWISH EMIGRATION

Getting the children to safety was one thing: moving their parents and other adults out of Germany was another. With the increasing closure of possible countries of refuge, Nazi authorities sought to find ways to facilitate Jewish emigration, such that obtaining all the necessary permissions required to leave could be streamlined.

In July 1938, *SS-Obersturmführer* Adolf Eichmann was given the task of accelerating Jewish emigration and easing the numerous bureaucratic bottlenecks through which aspiring emigrants had to pass (Stangneth, 2014). He adopted a centralized business model, ordering all relevant agencies to locate their offices in one place. He then also ordered the creation of a central Jewish organization so that he would have leaders with whom to negotiate.

The inception of the Central Office for Jewish Emigration (*Zentralstelle für jüdische Auswanderung*) resulted from Eichmann seeking an effective and efficient way of getting around the administrative logjam faced by Austrian Jews trying to leave Austria. His view was that because of the red tape of the various authorities, and particularly their lack of coordination, Jews who were prepared to emigrate found it extremely difficult to leave the country. For example, when the Revenue Office had issued the requisite certificate, an exit visa from the passport police might, in the meantime, have expired. It was because of such experiences that the Central Office for Jewish Emigration was set up.

The Central Office, in cooperation with other related government agencies, was to deal with the following matters:

- creating opportunities for emigration through negotiations for entry permits with the competent German and other emigration organizations;
- obtaining the foreign currency required for emigration;
- establishing and supervising professional retraining centers;
- cooperating with travel agencies and shipping companies to ensure the technical arrangements for emigration;
- supervising Jewish political and other emigration associations with regard to their attitude concerning emigration; and issuing guidelines and continuous contacts with all offices connected with the emigration of Jews from Austria.

All Nazi Party offices and other authorities were instructed to pass on all applications for emigration to the Central Office for Jewish Emigration immediately upon receipt without taking action of their own, and send to the Office all Jews desirous of emigrating. Jews wishing to emigrate were in the future to apply only to the Central Office for Jewish Emigration. The *Zentralstelle* was to control further procedures and, in particular, obtain the permits required for emigration from the competent office, and supervise the final emigration.

Eichmann had effectively established an "assembly line" system whereby a Jew could show up at the Central Emigration Office with his papers and proceed from desk to desk until he arrived at the end, with a passport and an exit visa but stripped of his property, cash, and rights, only a passport in which was written: "You must leave this country within two weeks; if you fail to do so, you will go to a concentration camp." Within a few months, the Office had processed the emigration of 150,000 Jews (Stangneth, 2014).

The Vienna office was founded in August 20, 1938, to overcome undesirable interruptions and delays occurring in Jewish emigration, and inefficiencies between offices when dealing with this increasing population movement. Eventually there was a network of these *Zentralstelle* institutions in Vienna, Prague, Berlin, and Amsterdam.

BYSTANDERS AND UPSTANDERS

During the Holocaust, a bystander was one who was at least aware of the perpetration of the Nazis' crimes but did nothing to halt them or to rescue Jews seeking help. In that regard, bystanders were neither perpetrators, collaborators, nor victims. Individuals and organizations (for example, the churches) became bystanders for various reasons. Some, for example, were hostile towards Jews though not sufficiently so as to want to carry out harmful actions against them. As in any society, some were simply apathetic with regard to what was happening to "the other." Some—often a majority—genuinely feared for their lives or those of their loved ones should there be repercussions for speaking out against the Nazi measures (and, even more so, for attempting to halt them). Further, the benefits that some people received through the dispossession and murder of the Jews added to the mix of why a person might stand by and not wish to get involved. There are, of course, many other reasons as to why bystanders did not speak out or act on the behalf of Jews.

Another category of bystander was those who knew what was happening, tried to inform the world of what they knew, but were helpless in their efforts. Take, for example, Gerhard Riegner, the Swiss representative of the World Jewish Congress, and author of the now-famous Riegner Telegram of August 29, 1942. Acting upon information received from a German industrialist who knew at first hand of Nazi plans for the extermination of the Jews, Riegner sent a cable to a number of Allied governments alerting Western leaders of Nazi plans—which, by that stage, were already well underway. The communication was sent to Rabbi Stephen S. Wise in the United States and Samuel Silverman, MP in Great Britain. Wise forwarded the cable to the U.S. State Department, after which months of delay ensured that no action was taken to save the lives of millions of Jews at that time being murdered in what was the most intensive period of sustained Nazi killing. From Switzerland, Riegner had to watch helplessly while this was being played out, in what was for him a time of immense and depressing frustration (Riegner, 2006).

The Holocaust illustrated the consequences of indifference and passivity towards the persecution of others. There could be little doubt that the vast majority of people in Germany and occupied Europe were aware, at least to some extent, of how the Nazi regime was treating the Jews, and bystanders were in the majority.

One of the many factors militating against action was ignorance. Nazi actions, though coordinated throughout the Reich, were not conveyed to the peoples over whom the Nazis ruled, and besides, the Nazis had effectively taken over all news outlets in Germany by the mid-1930s in any case. Citizens were exposed to extensive and persuasive propaganda in lieu of news. Within Germany, people could only act on the information they had available to them—and no-one, outside of a very few at the highest levels of the government, was fully aware of the big picture. Once war broke out in 1939, control over information became even tighter, and spread throughout occupied Europe. The Nazi regime used tactics of fear and terror to suppress any possibility of resistance or rescues, and for the most part (with a few important exceptions) any efforts to do so were only localized and not national in scale. All too often, moreover, there were no means to resist, and some bystanders were literally paralyzed with fear or helplessness.

A major concern in studies of bystander behavior relates to the question of why they remain passive; why they do not help when a fellow human being is facing a dangerous situation (Latané and Darley, 1970). By way of response, some have considered the question of apathy as being an important indicator of behavior: genocide thereby became possible through an unquestioning obedience to evil leaders. Yet bystanders were often more than just compliant citizens of Nazi Germany, Austria, or the German-speaking areas of the Reich; all too often they were also to be found in German-occupied countries, encouraged not to get involved by collaborationist governments and their church leaders.

Nevertheless, the pressures of being and remaining a bystander were too much for some people. The pressures of wartime—and, frequently, the intimacy of occupation—sometimes led those who had stood back to eventually become resisters or rescuers. At other times, through their actions in standing by, many became victims themselves, as in the case of those caught in reprisal roundups by Nazis. By trying to live their lives beyond the fray, adopting a life of "business as usual," and not appearing to be conspicuous, some bystanders in fact made targets of themselves through their very anonymity—another tragic dimension of inaction in the face of Nazi terror.

Individuals, groups, and entire nations were forced to make choices as to whether or not to resist the Nazis and rescue Jews (and other victims), and knowing about their persecution but deciding to remain silent often became a daily torment. The issues raised by such situations raised profound moral questions, though often people were under too much stress to consider them at the time: under what circumstances could injustice and Nazi violence be confronted? Further, knowing of this, was it possible to do anything so long as the injustice was sustained? As with all such moral questions, they were not easy to resolve, and had to be considered on a case-by-case, and individual-by-individual, basis.

An upstander, on the other hand, is the opposite of a bystander. For whatever reason, bystanders generally do not get involved in situations in which moral choices need to be made in relation to right and wrong. As a result, it is uncommon for them to act when confronted with the persecution or abuse of another. Upstanders, on the other hand, will intervene in some way, choosing to take positive action in the face of injustice or in situations where others need assistance. An upstander is one who "stands up" for a cause or belief when they could otherwise have chosen to do nothing; put this way, a bystander is passive and does nothing to help when someone needs it, becoming complicit in the state's actions, whereas an upstander actively defends those needing to be defended in opposition to the will of the state.

Saying no to the Nazis was a choice people made, and it took exceptional courage and commitment to do so. Were, therefore, those who acted as upstanders heroic? It is a difficult question to answer. Certainly, many (possibly most) did not see themselves that way. The acts in which they engaged did not have to take place on a grand scale in order to be effective. To be sure, there were *some* exceptionally brave acts on the part of *some* individuals, but it was really in myriad small ways that the worst excesses of the Holocaust could be resisted—refusing to acquiesce, turning a blind eye, or maintaining their commitment to the sanctity of human life.

Upstanders during the Holocaust, engaging in an enormous variety of helping activities, demonstrated that the intended victims of the Nazis could sometimes find ways out of this most awful of situations. It must always be remembered, however, that their actions, though outstanding examples of goodness in the face of genocidal evil, managed to save only a tiny proportion of those whose lives the Nazis already considered to be forfeit. Moreover, saving lives was difficult, and sometimes next to impossible. Those who hid Jews from the Nazis risked not only their own lives but those of their families—their wives, husbands, children, and parents. Depending on where one was located, people caught helping or hiding Jews were, more often than not, executed immediately—either on the spot, or later, in public as an example to others.

Further, many of the stories surrounding upstanders have gone unrecorded, for they might have died and their exploits were not recorded, or they did not record them, or see a need for them to be remembered. One of the reasons for this was because, in so many cases, such people did not feel as though, by acting to stop Nazi atrocities, they did anything special. For these people, their actions simply constituted what they refer to, over and over again, as "the right thing to do."

PERPETRATORS AS RESCUERS

In addition, there were some Germans in uniform—a very few—who sought to minimize Jewish suffering or even save lives. Possessed of a range of different motives, they were united by one thing: they chose to act when they could otherwise have done nothing. Members of the perpetrator regime who hid Jews risked their own lives and sometimes those of their families under the principle of *sippenhaft* (a legal practice in Nazi Germany whereby relatives of those accused of crimes against the state were held to be equally responsible, and arrested and sometimes executed) (Loeffel, 2012). Given the enormous risks involved in undertaking rescue efforts, it is remarkable that any of these initiatives took place at all. And not only this; sometimes they aligned themselves with elements of Nazism, and in certain cases had joined the Nazi Party of their own volition earlier. Others saw themselves as fellow travelers but were selective when it came to persecution of Jews, or civilians, or simply had a commitment to the sanctity of human life.

Five quick examples can illustrate the activities of such people—all too often, conflicted Nazis who compromised their oath of loyalty to Hitler and the Third Reich by standing up for the higher moral principle of saving lives.

Hans Calmeyer was a renowned German lawyer who utilized his position within the Nazi regime to save thousands of Jews (Paldiel, 2000). Known in some circles as the "Dutch Schindler," he was neither Jewish nor did he have an ulterior motive for saving Jews besides his own moral code. In his role as an examiner of so-called "racial cases" in the occupied Netherlands, he ruled on appropriate classifications, adjudging whether those being examined were fully Jewish, partly Jewish, or Aryan, in accordance with Nazi legislation. He responded by falsifying Jewish identities, and through his efforts at least 3,000 Jewish lives were saved.

Hans Münch was an SS doctor stationed at Auschwitz, where he undertook research at the SS Hygiene Institute with a focus on bacteriological investigations of typhus (Lifton, 1986; Cernyak-Spatz, 2000). He carried out human experiments on concentration camp inmates but insisted that the only experiments to which he would agree would be non-life threatening. And, while all doctors at Auschwitz had to perform the duty of being present at selections when Jewish prisoners arrived, he refused (and was not punished). Then, when the end of the war was approaching in 1945, he provided a gun and the means to escape for the Jewish prisoners with whom he had been working in his research laboratory at Dachau.

Karl Plagge was a German military officer who joined the National Socialist Party in 1931 out of a conviction that the Nazi social and economic platform offered prosperity for Germany's future. In July 1941 he was sent to Vilna (Vilnius) commanding an engineering unit; once there, he witnessed severe anti-Jewish measures, and was conscience-stricken by what he saw. He thereupon decided to try to help Jews in the ghetto through the granting of life-saving work certificates. He issued some 250 such permits, covering about a thousand men, women, and children, between 1941 and mid-1944. At the same time, he obtained extra food rations, warm clothing, medical supplies, and firewood for his workers. Overall, it has been estimated that he saved up to 1,240 Jewish lives (Good, 2005).

Anton Schmid, an Austrian soldier serving in the Wehrmacht during World War II, saved Jews and was executed as a result (Silver, 1992). Like Plagge, he was stationed near Vilna, in this case working at the train station where he saw persecution of Jews at first hand. Repulsed by what he saw, he took Jews off trains, employed them as workers, arranged releases, and sheltered them when he could not facilitate their escape. Although he saved up to 250 men, women, and children, he was caught in the act and executed for treason on April 13, 1942.

Finally, the case of Kurt Gerstein is also worthy of note in the current context (Friedländer, 1969; Joffroy, 1971). An SS officer and member of the Waffen-SS Institute for Hygiene with responsibility for the delivery of large quantities of Zyklon B gas canisters to Auschwitz and other camps, on August 17, 1942, he went to Bełżec death camp, where he witnessed the gassing of some 3,000 Jews; the next day he went to Treblinka and saw a repetition of the killing process. Deeply disturbed by what he had seen, he was desperate to unburden himself, and in the weeks and months that followed he related all he had seen to as many people in positions of authority from neutral countries as he could. By April 1945, as defeat loomed for the Third Reich, he surrendered to the Allies. Transferred to Paris, he wrote his final account, now known as the Gerstein Report, in which he made a full disclosure of what he had witnessed as an SS officer. On July 25, 1945, he was found hanged in his cell—some said by suicide, others that he was murdered by Nazis imprisoned with him.

Anti-Nazi resistance, whether from those in uniform or those working for the regime, was usually focused more on opposition to the Nazi government than specific condemnations of Nazi anti-semitism—but denying the Nazis the chance to realize their murderous goals saw some people seeking to save lives under threat, through rescue (Schmid, Plagge), raising awareness (Gerstein), or in other ways such as concealment. They all had their reasons for acting as they did, and they all severely compromised their formal duty to the state—a duty to which they had taken an oath to uphold. Shared among them was the conflict they faced between their oath and their decision to undermine it through their actions. Others who chose to resist or stand against the regime did not have to deal with this conflict, rendering the decisions made by these conflicted Nazis perhaps even more impressive.

One can inquire whether, in taking their oath to serve the state (as everyone had to), they commited themselves to the Nazi regime in full knowledge and acceptance of the Nazi position regarding the treatment of the Jews—but changed their stance after seeing what it represented face to face (Münch). Or did they oppose the Nazi position even before they committed themselves to the regime, thinking, perhaps, that the best way to help mitigate the suffering was to do so "from the inside" (Gerstein, Calmeyer)? Put more simply, how did they reconcile their oath and their actions?

A further question to be asked of all those in this position is whether they were troubled by violating their oath, or did their moral convictions move them quickly beyond any such concerns? In order to approach this question, we need to resolve whether or not there was anything qualitatively different about their decision—given their position within the perpetrator regime—to resist or rescue, as compared to the decision of others who did so from the outside?

For all of them, it is clear, a higher duty beckoned. In their situation, the conflict between legality and morality was one that could probably not have been resolved, meaning that they had to choose—and in this, perhaps, for all of them at one time or another, is to be found the essence of their personal anguish.

INTERNATIONAL REACTIONS DURING THE WAR YEARS

Once war broke out in September 1939, the Allies were keen to find ways to paint their enemy in the worst possible light, and they used

Bermuda Conference was viewed as more of a public relations exercise than a serious attempt to address the issue.

On another level, alternative approaches to assisting Europe's Jews saw requests to bomb the rail lines leading to Auschwitz (and even the camp itself), and a somewhat bizarre offer from Adolf Eichmann to "sell" the Jews of Hungary to the Allies, late in the war, in what became known later as the "Blood for Goods" scheme (Weisberg, 1958; Bauer, 1996). Only in 1944, under pressure both inside and outside his government, did President Roosevelt call into being the War Refugee Board which, ultimately, was responsible for the saving of 200,000 lives though not, for the most part, through emigration to the United States (Wyman, 1984; Breitmann and Lichtman, 2013).

While the record of Allied governments in saving Jews was, on the whole, poor, international bodies such as the Roman Catholic Church and the International Committee of the Red Cross were hardly better—though both organizations have worked hard since 1945 to rebuild their reputations.

At the Vatican, Pope Pius XII, who was intensely opposed to communism, theologically conservative, and disposed towards Germanophilia, repeatedly refused to offer any public condemnation of the Nazi assault against the Jews. Some have argued that his public silence and failure to speak out, given his position as the acknowledged moral voice of the Western world's conscience, could possibly have lessened the tragedy. His supporters, on the other hand, hold that the actions of the Vatican to give comfort and succor to Jews, much of it in secret, were all done with the Pope's knowledge and support (Cornwell, 1999; Zuccotti, 2000).

The International Committee of the Red Cross (ICRC), on the other hand, which also had a huge role to play internationally as the world's premier humanitarian organization, did not issue a public appeal on behalf of the Jews, claiming that its policies of neutrality, impartiality, and confidentiality had to be measured against whatever good it was capable of doing—and what the effect would be if it was denied access to prisons, detention centers, concentration camps and the like during the war (Favez, 1999). The ICRC's ability to see to its core tasks—monitoring of prisoner conditions, carrying messages between the Jewish Question as a means to do this. Still, they did not extend their own efforts to helping rescue Jews. The preference was always to assert that the best way to help those being persecuted was to win the war, and that no other distraction could be allowed to stand in the way of achieving that objective.

On December 17, 1942, by which time Nazi Germany had deported more than 2 million Jews to death camps (and perhaps up to a million had been murdered by *Einsatzgruppen* and police battalions), a joint statement was made simultaneously in London, Washington, and Moscow condemning the Nazi mass murder of the Jews. The statement specifically identified that the crimes being described were targeting Jews—not Allied nationals or citizens, but, explicitly, Jews. Second, the Allies promised to punish those perpetrating the crimes identified. And third, they had no hesitation in employing the word "extermination" to describe what they had by that stage categorized. Such condemnation, the most damning indictment issued against Nazi mass murder to date, was in fact to be the only multilateral denunciation of German actions towards the Jews throughout the duration of the Holocaust. Before this time and subsequently, no other inter-Allied declaration mentioned the Nazi extermination in this manner.

Jewish hopes were buoyed by the announcement, however, and at another conference, convened by Britain and the United States and held in Bermuda on April 19, 1943, some anticipated that definite action on behalf of the Jews would follow (Penkower, 1983; Wyman, 1984). The supposed purpose of the Bermuda Conference was to discuss the Jewish plight, but, held at this remote site in order to control the flow of information by the news media, no official representatives of Jewish organizations were permitted to attend, and the agenda was severely curtailed. The particularity of Jewish suffering was masked by use of the term "political refugees." The Conference placed more emphasis on prisoners of war than on refugees; the possibility of Palestine as a site for refugees, then under British control, was not discussed; there was no debate entered into regarding any direct negotiations between the Allies and Germany; and even discussions of sending food parcels to those already incarcerated in the concentration camps was curtailed. At its conclusion, on May 1, 1943, th prisoners and their families, advocating more humane conditions, providing food and other "comforts" for prisoners, delivering emergency aid to victims of armed conflicts, among others—was put under immense strain during the Holocaust, when the ICRC's mandate did not extend to civilian prisoners. Many critics, however, have argued that during the Holocaust the ICRC failed to live up to its core mandate of serving populations in danger (Ben-Tov, 1988; Favez, 1999).

Overall, one of the key questions coming from the Holocaust must be whether or not Allied actions—beyond winning the war—could have prevented the Holocaust or reduced the number of those murdered by the Nazis and those supporting them in occupied Europe. While there is no easy answer to this because things did not work out that way, there can be little doubt that the silence and inaction of the world community resulted in the avoidable loss of countless lives.

DISCUSSION QUESTIONS

- Did the United States and other countries fail to rescue Jews during the Holocaust?
- Was the Evian Conference of 1938 a failure? How can this be measured?
- Those identified as Righteous among the Nations often reject the idea that they should be recognized for having done anything special. How would you respond to such a position?
- What were some of the factors hindering rescue activities within Nazi Europe?
- Could it be said that the nations of the outside world abandoned the Jews to their fate? Explain your response through reference to the policies of specific countries.

RESISTANCE DURING THE HOLOCAUST

OVERVIEW

What constituted resistance during the Holocaust? There were many forms of refusal to comply with the regime, ranging from armed confrontation to a passive defiance that simply sought to maintain dignity and a sense of what it meant to be human. Resistance also embraced those who sought to save lives, through rescue, concealment, or any other means of denying the Nazis the chance to realize their murderous goals.

In Germany, most Jews were taken completely by surprise by the vehemence of Nazi antisemitism, uncompromising in the level of its hatred and violence. After the previous century, in which Jews became more and more integrated into mainstream German life, the Nazi assault overwhelmed them like the eruption of Vesuvius. For the majority, it took years before they understood that they no longer had a future in a country they considered to be their home.

Opposition of any sort, accordingly, was slow in coming. One of the first statements came from the editor of the national Jewish newspaper *Jüdische Rundschau*, Robert Welstch, who responded to the Nazi-inspired, nation-wide boycott of all Jewish businesses on April 1, 1933, by writing an editorial—"Wear the Yellow Badge with Pride!"—which was a display of Jewish assertiveness in the face of Nazi provocation (Dippel, 1996).

At other times, particularly during the war years, anti-Nazi resistance surfaced, but it was more in the way of opposition to the Nazi regime than condemnations of the Holocaust. In 1942, for example, a Jewish anti-Nazi group led by Herbert Baum and his wife Marianne was active. For their attempt to disrupt a Nazi propaganda exhibition in Berlin in 1942 they were executed (Brothers, 2012). So also were the leading members of the Christian anti-Nazi group, the White Rose, who wrote and distributed pamphlets condemning the regime one year later (Dumbach and Newborn, 2007; Hanser, 2012).

World War II began with the German invasion of Poland on September 1, 1939. Before the month was out Nazi antisemitic measures had begun in the occupied areas, and during the months that followed Jews were herded into ghettos. With persecution eventually came a response, particularly from Jewish youth. One of the first revolts took place in the ghetto of Łachwa in September 1942 after a resistance movement had been formed under the leadership of Dov Lopatyn and Isaac Rochczyn (Bartrop, 2016). This was but a start. In ghettos throughout Poland, Lithuania, Belorussia, and Ukraine, resistance movements emerged—some more slowly than others, but extending throughout the entire region. Perhaps a hundred ghettos spawned underground movements of one sort or another (see "Other Forms of Resistance," below).

The most famous of these included Vilna, where the *Fareynikte Partizaner Organizatsie* (United Partisan Organization, or FPO) was led by Abba Kovner; Minsk, where the resistance was led by Mihail Gebelev and Hersh Smolar; and Białystok, where the resistance movement was led by Daniel Moskowitz and Mordechaj Tenenbaum, who had formed the *Antyfaszystowska Organizacja Bojowa* (Anti-Fascist Military Organisation, or AOB) (Bartrop, 2016). Unquestionably, however, the ghetto resistance best known was the Warsaw Ghetto Uprising of April–May, 1943 (see p. 000).

In the Nazi extermination camps, too, resistance was also mounted. The most celebrated of these, as we shall see, were large-scale prisoner rebellions at Treblinka, Sobibór, and Auschwitz. Other expressions of resistance also took place elsewhere in the Nazi ghettos and concentration camps.

Taken collectively, resistance was an active, ongoing process of opposition to all aspects of life as intended by the Nazis. It could take many forms, and arise over any issue. It was as much an attitude as a physical process, and sought to negate the commands, rules, intentions, actions, statements, and deprivations imposed by the SS. Its numerous forms enabled men and women to take some measure of control over their fate in an environment in which survival and success were in no sense guaranteed. Every act of helping, encouragement, and cooperation that took place disproved the claim that an attitude of self-reliance could not be maintained, and individuals, groups, and resistance movements all sought to establish and maintain this attitude.

Beyond the ghettos and camps, partisan groups comprised of guerrilla fighters risked their lives through fighting Nazis, particularly in the forests of eastern Poland, Ukraine, and Belorussia. They attacked railroads, bridges, and military installations, but sometimes also cared for non-military combatants—women and children, or those too young, too old, or too sick to fight. Among the most high profile of the partisan groups was that associated with the Bielski brothers, Tuvia, Asael, Zus, and Aron. Other operational commanders included Icheskel Atlas in the Lipiczanska Forest; Moshe Gildenman ("Uncle Misha") in the Volhynia region of Ukraine; and a remarkable woman, Eta Wrobel, who commanded a Jewish partisan unit in the forests of central Poland.

In all cases, partisan military operations were essentially based around sabotage and guerrilla tactics rather than direct confrontation. Partisans were mainly active in Eastern Europe, especially after the Nazi invasion of the Soviet Union in the summer of 1941, and their activities ranged widely across Nazi-occupied Europe, extending to France, Belgium, and other places as well as Eastern Europe.

Physical defiance was the most obvious manifestation of resistance, but spiritual resistance was also paramount—as secret religious observance, artistic and creative endeavors, teaching and learning, and disseminating news. In other contexts, Jews helped each other to escape the Nazis through arranging illegal border crossings, smuggling, forging papers to create false identities, and hiding, sometimes for years.

One of the greatest myths of the Holocaust is that the Jews made little or no effort to defend themselves against their Nazi oppressors, as clearly resistance did take place and took many forms.

PARTISANS DURING THE HOLOCAUST

It has been estimated that anywhere between 20,000 and 30,000 Jewish men and women fought as partisans against the Nazis and their allies during World War II (Ainsztein, 1974). Their military operations were essentially sabotage and guerrilla tactics rather than direct confrontation due to their small numbers in any given location, coupled with their limited supplies of weapons, food, and medicine.

Most partisan resistance took place after 1942, once it became clear that the Nazis were murdering every Jew in Europe. Partisan movements were most numerous in the occupied countries of Eastern Europe, where Jews resisted both as individuals and in groups. Armed units operated in Ukraine, Belorussia, Lithuania, Poland, and Russia, among other places, and often formed an important component of local resistance operations (Tec, 2013). In Lithuania, for example, Jews made up approximately 10 percent of the partisan units (Greenbaum, 1997).

In Western Europe, Jewish resistance units were established in France and Belgium, where they would engage in clandestine military operations or help their fellow Jews escape across nearby borders. Jews also fought alongside other partisans in Greece, Italy, Yugoslavia, and the Netherlands.

The vast majority had been civilians before the war, and most were young, with prewar Jewish youth groups forming the foundation for much of the resistance activity taking place in the forests and ghettos. Resistance fighters usually ranged in age from their late teens to about twenty-five, while children also sometimes bore arms. In the normal run of events, most partisan units were small, numbering only a few dozen fighters. Very few had any prior military training, though some, who had served in the Polish or Soviet armies, formed a useful leadership cohort in the areas of strategy and military know-how.

As forces that emerged informally, with little to no training and no entrenched leadership, partisan groups faced great obstacles. Lack of armaments, conducting operations in a hostile zone, and civilian backgrounds were important factors militating against large-scale operations, but many fighters were also plagued by a reluctance to leave their families behind and a fear of reprisals, together with the ever-present Nazi terror—to say nothing of concerns about their own personal security in a combat situation for which they were underprepared. These anxieties were further compounded by trying to operate in what was often an already-hostile antisemitic environment from among local people who were, in many cases, their prewar neighbors.

While in some places Jewish partisans received assistance from local villagers, they could not rely on the possibility that they would be supported, partly because of widespread antisemitism and partly because of local fears of punishment should those providing aid be caught helping. Partisans lived in constant danger of informers revealing their whereabouts to the Germans. Further, to avoid the ever-present risk of discovery, every unit was either always moving or had to be prepared to do so at a moment's notice.

Given this, secrecy and concealment were paramount, and as a result most partisan groups were frequently cut off from the world. Other than through learning what was happening elsewhere from captured prisoners, newly arrived fighters, or occasional contacts with other partisan groups, they often knew little of what was happening in the wider world or the war.

On the positive side, however, geography and topography favored the kind of warfare in which the partisans were able to engage, mounting hit-and-run raids prior to disappearing back into the densely wooded areas or swamps from where they based their operations. Over time, many Jewish groups in Eastern Europe were absorbed into the command structure of the much larger Soviet partisan movement, but even here antisemitism and discrimination were frequent.

Jewish partisan groups often moved beyond fighting or sabotage, and sometimes sheltered families, women, and children, working to protect Jewish lives at this time of greatest threat. As a result, some groups could number in the hundreds, though operating with only a small actual fighting strength. These family camps usually consisted of escapees from ghettos or those fleeing from villages in advance of the occupation, and acted as sites—insecure, to be sure—where those too young or too old to fight hoped to wait out the war.

Fighters in the ghettos and concentration camps, even though not in the forests, can also be considered as partisans, even though they enjoyed much less freedom of action than those outside. In many concentration camps in Germany, Poland, and elsewhere—and in death camps such as Sobibór, Treblinka, and Auschwitz, for example—large-scale prisoner revolts took place, resulting in huge losses of life but the destruction of the Nazis' murder machinery.

It wasn't easy being a partisan, and the life was demanding at all times. It required extraordinary bravery and cunning as well as the ability to withstand challenging living conditions. Finding adequate shelter, especially in winter, was always a challenge. Moreover, even simple activities such as lighting fires for warmth had to be curtailed, out of fear that the smoke would reveal their location. Pinpointing food sources was an ongoing trial, and sometimes the partisans had to resort to force or theft to obtain sustenance from farmers and villagers. Many partisans were either unarmed or very lightly armed, and lived in constant fear of enemy patrols. And the threat of German reprisals was ever-present, since retribution for partisan acts targeted civilians in substantial numbers.

After the war, the fighting partisans, whether in forests, ghettos, or camps, became the symbol of Jewish resistance to Nazi tyranny, though there were, of course, many other ways in which resistance activities could take place without a reliance on armed force. In fact, in order to survive it was often better not to fight back—though every situation had to be assessed on its merits, and when looking at the situation today the time-and-place circumstances of all resistance activities must always be taken into account (see Box 6.1).

BOX 6.1 PORTRAIT OF A RESISTER: ETA WROBEL

Eta Wrobel was a commander of Jewish partisans in the forests of central Poland during the Holocaust. Born Eta Chajt into a solidly middle class family of ten in Łuków, eastern Poland on December 28, 1916, in early 1940, soon after the war began, she began working as a clerk in an employment agency, but quickly began her resistance activities by creating false identity papers for Jews in the work office set up by German Reserve Police Battalion 101 in Łuków. She also smuggled guns she had stolen from Nazis in Łódź, and somehow got them to Łuków. She was, however, eventually denounced and arrested by the Gestapo.

Imprisoned in Lublin, she was beaten and tortured in order to divulge the names of other resisters. She held out for ten months, before being released for work duties building the death camp at nearby Majdanek. This was highly unusual, as Jews were at no time ever permitted to do such work, but Eta had assistance from outside the prison through the intervention of the family of another prisoner. On the way to the worksite, she managed to slip away from the wagon on which she was riding, and ran into the forest. Here, she was met by her father, who had escaped the destruction of the Łuków ghetto.

The ghetto had been established in May 1941, and was destroyed before the end of 1942. By then the population had grown to nearly 12,000. Deportations, mainly to Treblinka, took place in early October and early November, while some 2,200 Jews were shot into pits locally . Whatever remained of the ghetto was transformed into a slave labor camp, but over the next few months thousands of those who had survived the initial deportations, and others who had been relocated there from elsewhere, were shot dead or transported to Treblinka. Only about 150 Jews of Łuków survived the Holocaust.

Under these circumstances, it was ironic that Eta could count herself as one of the survivors of the Łuków ghetto, given that she had already been imprisoned by the Gestapo. Having fled to the woods, she then helped organize an all-Jewish partisan unit numbering about eighty, which, because of innate military skills, she ultimately commanded. She was active on missions with men, and made important strategic decisions under which the unit would steal German supplies, set mines, and engage in skirmishing.

The unit lived rough. They slept in cramped quarters, and had no access to medical attention. Unlike the other seven women in the unit, she refused to cook or clean. On one mission Eta was shot in the leg, and went to see a friendly Polish doctor. The bullet was difficult to remove, and he kept asking her to come back when the swelling went down. This only led to intense pain and sustained swelling over several months, so eventually the doctor gave her a knife and a bottle of alcohol, and she dug the bullet out herself. It was said that the experience she gained from this was beneficial in other ways, as she then learned how to remove bullets from wounded fellow partisans.

In July 1944 the Soviet Army liberated Łuków. Eta came out of hiding, and was asked if she was interested in becoming the mayor of Łuków. She readily accepted this on the grounds that by doing so she could make a positive difference for the future. On December 20, 1944, she was married, and in 1947 she and her husband, Henry, moved to the United States, settling first in Brooklyn before moving to New Jersey. They raised three children, who in turn produced nine grandchildren. Eta, for her part, was the only child in a family of ten to survive the Holocaust.

After settling in the United States, Eta spent much of her time engaging in community activities such as raising money to assist in anti-cancer initiatives. In later life she traveled throughout New Jersey educating schoolchildren about her experiences, and generally imparting to them a lifetime of accumulated wisdom wrung from the most testing of conditions. In 2006, at the age of 90, she wrote her memoirs, a book entitled *My Life My Way*.

Eta Wrobel died on May 26, 2008, in Highland, New York, at the age of 92. Before her death, she summarized her years with the partisans by saying, "The biggest resistance that we could have done to the Germans was to survive" (Wrobel, 2006; Bartrop, 2016).

A CELEBRATED CASE: THE BIELSKI PARTISANS

Jewish partisan groups fighting the Nazis in the forests of Belarus, Ukraine, and Poland, as we have seen, faced considerable obstacles to both survival and success. One celebrated case among many is that of Tuvia Bielski and his brothers Asael, Alexander (known as Zus), and Aron (Tec, 1993; Duffy, 2003).

The children of David and Beila Bielski from a family of twelve children (ten boys and two girls), they were the only Jews in Stankiewicze, a small village then situated in eastern Poland, between the towns of Lida and Novogródek (Navahrudak). Born in 1906, Tuvia Bielski could speak Polish, Yiddish, and German. Recruited into the Polish Army in 1927, after demobilization he married and became a store owner in the small town of Subotniki, which was occupied by the Soviets in September 1939. With the Nazi invasion in June 1941 Tuvia, Zus, and Asael were called up for home defense against the invaders. In early July 1941 the Nazis moved Jews from across the region into a ghetto in Nowogródek, but the Bielski brothers went into hiding instead; after they learned that the rest of the family had been killed in the ghetto in late 1941, they fled into the forest.

Together with thirteen neighbors who had also survived the initial Nazi assault, they established the nucleus of a partisan combat group in the spring of 1942. Originally this consisted of some forty people, but it grew quickly once word got around that the group refused to turn away Jews.

In the forest, however, there was a great deal of uncertainty. Should they fight back through joining a partisan unit, or create one of their own? And what form would such fighting take? Further, what would be the objectives of such a unit? Eventually the Bielskis established a community of fighters which also cared for non-military combatants—those considered too young, too old, or too sick to fight.

As the commander of what became known as the "Bielski *otriad*" (partisan detachment), Tuvia's priority was to save Jews rather than kill Germans, and in pursuit of this he sent emissaries to infiltrate ghettos in the area and recruit new members to join the group in the Naliboki Forest. Hundreds of men, women, and children, individually or in small groups, eventually found their way to the Bielski camp. At its peak 1,236 people belonged to the *otriad*, with up to 70 percent of its membership consisting of women, children, and the elderly. Fewer than 200 actually engaged in armed operations.

The partisan community was housed in underground dugouts (*zemlyankas*) or bunkers. In addition, several utility structures were built: a kitchen, a mill, a bakery, a bathhouse, a medical clinic for the sick and wounded, and a quarantine hut for those who suffered from infectious diseases such as typhus. A small herd of cows supplied milk. Artisans made goods and carried out repairs, providing the combatants with logistical support that later served Soviet partisan units in the vicinity as well. More than 125 workers toiled in the workshops, which became famous among partisans far beyond the Bielski base: tailors patched up old clothing and stitched together new garments; shoemakers attended to footwear; and leather workers labored on belts, bridles, and saddles. A metalworking shop repaired damaged weapons and constructed new ones from spare parts. A tannery, constructed to produce the hide for cobblers and leather workers, became a makeshift synagogue in which several of the tanners, observant Jews, could pray. Carpenters, hatmakers, barbers, and watchmakers served the community, nicknamed "Bielsk" in honor of the leadership. The camp's many children attended class in a *zemlyanka* set up as a school. The camp even had its own jail and rudimentary court of law.

The Bielski group's partisan activities were aimed at the Nazis and their collaborators, such as Belorussian volunteer policemen or local inhabitants who had betrayed or killed Jews. They also conducted sabotage missions.

In 1943 the Nazis led major clearing operations against all partisan groups in the area, with some groups suffering major casualties. The Bielski partisans, however, fled safely to a more remote and impenetrable part of the forest, and continued to offer protection to noncombatants. They raided nearby villages to seize food (much like most other partisan groups), and on occasion locals who refused to share were subjected to violence, generating hostility towards the partisans from peasants in the villages.

The Bielski partisans eventually became affiliated with Soviet organizations in the Naliboki Forest. Several attempts by Soviet partisan commanders to absorb Bielski fighters into their own units were resisted, and under Tuvia's command the Bielski *otriad* retained its separate identity. This allowed him to continue protecting Jewish lives as well as engaging in combat. According to partisan documentation, Bielski fighters overall killed a total of 381 enemy troops, sometimes during joint actions with Soviet groups. Only fifty members who sought protection with the Bielski *otriad* did not survive.

TWO FRENCH MOVEMENTS: THE *ARMÉE JUIVE* AND THE MJS

As in most cases of persecution, there were some among the Jewish population within occupied France who were not prepared to accept their victimization passively. From an early date one such group, created by a few committed Zionists, became arguably the leading Jewish resistance organization and a focus for other opposition bodies throughout France (Lazare, 1996).

Abraham Polonski was one of the founders of this movement. Like many others, he was of immigrant background. Born in Russia in 1913, he moved to France before World War II. Here, he worked as an electrical engineer in Toulouse, and in August 1940, after the French surrender, he and his wife Eugénie, together with Dovid Knut and his wife Ariane, and (Aron) Lucien Lublin, came together to build a secret underground organization called *La Main Forte* (The Strong Hand). Its aim was to establish a movement that would defeat the Germans prior to moving on to Palestine where they would work to establish a Jewish state (Latour, 1981; Lazare, 1996).

Dovid Knut (born Duvid Meerovich Fiksman) was born in 1900 in Orgeev (Orhei), Bessarabia—the Romanian-speaking region of Russia (now Moldova). The son of a grocer, and from an observant Jewish family, he was raised in Kishinev (Chişinău). Having developed an early interest in poetry, at the age of fourteen he began publishing his poems and by 1918 was editing the magazine *Molodaya mysl'* (*Young Thought*). In 1920 he moved to Paris, where he took several odd jobs while learning French by night at the *Alliance Française*.

In late 1934, having divorced his first wife, Sarra Groboys, Knut began a relationship with Ariane Scriabina, daughter of the Russian composer Alexander Scriabin. Ariane associated herself with the Russian émigré community and married Knut, who would be her third husband. In 1940 Ariane converted to Judaism and took the name Sarah, demanding that she be called by only that name from then on. Her conversion was viewed as a betrayal by the non-Jewish Russian immigrant community, but for Ariane her identification with the Jewish people became an obsession. She became intolerant of even the slightest manifestations of antisemitism, a characteristic that would condition her and Knut's attitude towards Nazism once France had been overrun in 1940.

Shortly before the country fell and the Germans entered Paris, Ariane joined Knut in Toulouse. It was here, on January 10, 1942, that they joined with Abraham Polonski (whose resistance code names were "Mr. Pol" and "Maurice Ferrer") and the others to establish an underground Jewish militia, the *Armée Juive* (Jewish Army, or AJ). The first members of the AJ were recruited from a Torah study group led by a Polish-born rabbi in Toulouse, Paul Roitman, and initially they assisted with supplying the inmates of internment camps attempting to escape in and around Toulouse. The organization received funds from a refugee group based in Switzerland, the Zionist Organization of France.

Armée Juive activities were directed essentially by Polonski and Lublin and undertaken by the most committed members of the various Zionist youth movements. Through to the summer of 1942, Polonski and Lublin recruited militants from Toulouse, Montpellier, Nice, Grenoble, Lyon, and Limoges. They, in turn, fought in their own cities as well as Paris, attacking informers and Gestapo collaborators.

The intentions of the AJ were twofold: to protect Jews threatened by the Nazis, and to develop military skills that could then be used to help in the establishment of a Jewish state in Palestine. The Zionist background of the members was important here; Abraham and Eugénie Polonski had been strongly influenced by the right-wing Zionist Revisionist movement of Vladimir Jabotinsky, advocating belligerency and assertiveness. As the war progressed, the AJ's peak strength eventually numbered some 2,000 fighters. Recruitment standards were severe, with secrecy and obedience mandatory. The primary purpose of the organization was to resist when success seemed likely, as well as rescuing Jews by the provision of false papers, assisting with border crossings, and the like.

The *Armée Juive* was comprised, for the most part, of young Jews who had decided to take their defense into their own hands.

Recruitment was secret, passed by word of mouth and through friends recommending friends, always with the utmost regard to security and double-checking of authenticity. At all costs, the danger of denunciation had to be reduced to a minimum, and to preserve secrecy even further AJ action groups were deliberately kept small.

The city of Montpellier, located near the south coast of France just over 100 miles from Marseille, was the location in May 1942 of a conference of Jewish resisters that saw the establishment of the United Zionist Youth Movement (*Mouvement de la jeunesse sioniste*, or MJS) (Iancu, 2008). This was the culmination of an effort made by Simon Lévitte, a French Jew born in Ekaterinoslav, Russia (modern-day Dnipro, Ukraine), who had moved to Wiesbaden, Germany in 1922 prior to emigrating to Palestine with his wife. They returned to France with the task of organizing youth migration back to Palestine. In 1942 Lévitte started liaising between the occupied and Vichy zones, and after several shuttles he was successful in establishing rescue networks across numerous existing Jewish youth organizations. The MJS was one of these. Montpellier, a university city, contained a large concentration of refugee students, and now emerged as the location of a new type of resistance presence, tougher and more intense than some of the earlier groups had been (Iancu, 2008). After a short period, the MJS moved its operational base from Montpellier to Grenoble.

The MJS, true to its Zionist origins, began with a specific focus of providing young Jewish men and women with the educational, physical, and vocational training that would equip them for life in Palestine. Perhaps not surprisingly, given this, many members of the MJS were at one and the same time members of the *Armée Juive*. Having moved to Grenoble, they began low-level underground activities such as placing anti-Nazi posters and painting messages on walls. With direction from Simon Lévitte and Jules ("Dika") Jefroykin, they learned other activities as well: the intensification of anti-Jewish measures meant they were forced to undertake relief work and resistance through the creation of a Jewish documentation center that forged false papers, ration cards, and other life-saving documents. Among the young people who made contributions was a former refugee from Germany, Marianne Cohn. In the forging operations in and around Moissac, she became coordinating secretary for the organization.

In April 1943, Simon Lévitte went to Brussels, where he recruited Paul Giniewski, a young Viennese-born member of the Zionist movement. His brother, Otto ("Toto") Giniewski, was to prove the MJS's master forger, organizing the false papers department in Grenoble. Paul traveled throughout the region seeking friendly mayors and other officials prepared to provide current blank registration forms and identity cards, before searching for engravers and printers willing to provide counterfeit official stamps and then print the forms thereby created. It was extremely risky work for Paul, made even more dangerous as he then had to transport the material to and from his brother's "factory" at Seyssins, not far from Grenoble. After this, the false documents had to be conveyed throughout the region, so they could be distributed to their intended recipients.

The MJS also began finding ways to smuggle Jews away from the danger zones. While moving people to Switzerland and Spain was the ideal solution, in many cases the most that could be hoped for was removal to safer areas within France to await a further transfer later. This, of course, presented problems—the most important of which included identifying the means to transport them secretly, a place to which they could be removed (and sustained, possibly for an indeterminate period), and, should an opportunity be presented, finding a way to smuggle them across the border and a guide to assist them as they went.

Money presented a huge problem. Sustaining those in flight was a costly affair, as many of those helping from outside the networks required payment in return for the hazardous work in which they were engaged. Where people were housed for any period, their upkeep had to be paid for as well—and this was more expensive in the cities than outside metropolitan areas. Consequently, rescue activities often had to be accompanied by fundraising activities to pay off those who were putting themselves and their families at risk by harboring Jews or arranging for them to be smuggled from one location to another. And, by the time the refugees reached the border, local *passeurs* often charged very large sums for their assistance; too often, it was far from given freely.

OTHER FORMS OF RESISTANCE

Resistance during World War II took on many different forms and occurred on a scale ranging from countless individual acts of resistance to large, well-organized resistance movements. In every nation occupied by German or Axis forces there was some level of resistance, both by Jews and non-Jews, and not just against military occupation. Many also resisted Nazi and fascist ideology. Resistance was most keenly felt in Eastern Europe and was largely (though far from exclusively) carried out by Jews. The number of resisters and resistance groups will likely never be known for certain, because many postwar governments tended to inflate the number of resisters for political reasons. In many places, resistance was not centrally organized; in fact, some resistance movements were badly fractured by ideological, political, and religious differences.

Resistance itself encompassed a wide array of active and passive measures. Active resistance included sabotage, murder, assassinations, intelligence-gathering, bombings, and the like. Passive resistance also took many forms. It included non-cooperation with authorities, civil disobedience, organizing underground newspapers, and hiding or smuggling Jews out of the country. Resistance, of course, also occurred via large-scale groups organized as military units.

Jewish spiritual resistance took on a multitude of forms. It ranged from creating Jewish institutions in ghettos and concentration camps to providing clandestine education for children. It also encompassed the observation of Jewish holidays and religious and cultural rituals, preserving the history of communal existence, maintaining journals and memoirs, and collecting and hiding documentation of Jewish experiences during World War II.

A significant Jewish resistance movement operated within Germany itself, much of it undertaken by Zionist groups such as *Hashomer Hatzair*. In the Netherlands, Jews participating in resistance activities operated closely with non-Jewish resisters, including the communists. No fewer than 1,000 Dutch Jews struggled against German occupation, though only half survived the war. Jewish resistance in Belgium increased once German occupation began in the late spring of 1940. Belgian resistance encompassed urban guerrilla-style warfare, including sabotage; it also involved hiding Belgian Jews. Between 1941 and 1945 at least 3,000 Belgian Jewish children were in hiding (Vromen, 2008). French Jews made up nearly 20 percent of the total French Resistance movement, even though Jews were only approximately 1 percent of the French population (Latour, 1981).

Many Jewish revolts took place in ghettos as well as in labor camps, concentration camps, and death camps. Large uprisings took place in ghettos between 1941 and 1945. French resistance to the German occupation, which began in June 1940, was considered as the most organized resistance movement during the war. Included in this were the (non-Jewish) Maquis, guerrilla-style fighters, and from 1943 the National Council of Resistance directed and coordinated the different movements of the French Resistance (Kedward, 1993). In February 1943 resisters in Norway attacked a hydroelectric plant and helped delay what seemed like pre-production of an atomic bomb (Gjelsvik, 1979). There were also many active resisters in the Soviet Union; they fought against the German occupation, mainly in the western portions of the country, and included Jews and non-Jews alike.

It is difficult to gauge the effectiveness of the resistance, or the extent to which these contributed to the defeat of the Germans and their allies. Yet resistance movements were successful in that they required that the Germans divert significant resources to stem subversion and locate resisters.

THE WARSAW GHETTO UPRISING

Throughout the summer of 1942, the Germans deported or executed more than 300,000 Jews from the Warsaw Ghetto, leaving between 55,000 to 60,000. With reports filtering back of mass killings of those who had been deported taking place, younger inhabitants of the ghetto formed the Jewish Fighting Organization (*Żydowska Organizacja Bojowa*, or ŻOB) with the intention of obstructing—indeed, of stopping—any further deportations. Initial military action took place in January 1943; shocked at the audacity of the Jews and unaware as to the fighters' strength, the Germans withdrew from the ghetto to regroup their forces and evaluate the situation (Gutman, 1994).

On the evening of April 19, 1943, corresponding to the first night of the Jewish holy season of Passover, German forces, under the command of General Jürgen Stroop, attempted to destroy the Warsaw Ghetto and its Jewish inhabitants as a next-day birthday present to Adolf Hitler. Much to the Germans' surprise, the ŻOB, learning of the German plans, and led by Mordecai Anielewicz, prepared to meet the invaders. With a Herculean guerrilla effort comprising only about 500 inexperienced fighters, and another 250 fighters attached to a separate group, the *Żydowski Związek Wojskowy* (Jewish Military Union, or ŻZW), they commenced their resistance effort.

The battle, beginning on April 19, lasted until May 16, an intense four-week period of often desperate hand-to-hand fighting, when the command bunker at Miła 18 was finally destroyed and the ŻOB leadership, including Anielewicz, were all killed (Gutman, 1994). (In a communiqué to another leader of the resistance movement, Yitzhak Zuckerman, dated April 23—who was at that time outside the ghetto trying desperately to secure assistance from non-Jewish Poles—Anielewicz wrote that "my life's dream has been realized: I have lived to see Jewish defense in the ghetto in all its greatness and glory" (Zuckerman, 1993)).

Prior to this final confrontation, given that the Germans were largely unsuccessful in killing the resisters in open combat, they resorted to the technique of burning down the houses and apartment buildings in the ghetto, street by street and block by block. By May 16, Stroop was able to report to his military commanders that "The Jewish Quarter of Warsaw is no more! More than 56,000 Jewish bandits have been captured" (Stroop, 1979; Moczarski, 1981). He compiled a detailed 75-page report with 69 pictures, along with communiqués relevant to the suppression of the uprising, covering the period April 24, 1943 to May 24, 1943. Bound in black leather and entitled *The Jewish Quarter of Warsaw Is No More!*, the report was intended as a souvenir album for Heinrich Himmler and Stroop's immediate superior, Friedrich Jeckeln. While not materially affecting either the outcome of the war itself or the Final Solution—indeed, no resistance movement was ever successful in doing so—the Warsaw Ghetto Uprising remains the symbol of Jewish resistance to Nazi tyranny.

THE CAMP REVOLTS

Resistance among concentration camp prisoners was at all times hazardous, and was never intended to defeat the Nazis. Auschwitz was a good example of this. It did not have the chance to develop a fully-fledged resistance movement from within; the decision to organize a secret resistance movement was taken in Warsaw in mid-1940, not long after the camp was established. A Polish cavalry reserve officer, Witold Pilecki, approached his superiors in the Secret Polish Army (*Tajna Armia Polska*) with a proposal that he go to Auschwitz as a volunteer and start a military underground movement there. He received permission to do so, let himself be taken prisoner in a Warsaw round-up, and arrived in Auschwitz on September 22, 1940, under an assumed name and with forged papers. To create his organization he reasoned that only a system based on the strictest secrecy could have any hope of success. He named his secret network the Union of Military Organization (Pilecki, 2012).

At the same time Pilecki was establishing his resistance movement, another was being formed by Stanislaw Dubois under the direction of the Polish Socialist Party. Within a short time, a third group was formed by right-wing Polish nationalist elements. It was not until December 1941 that the three groups came together in some sort of federated movement, but by that stage it was not representative of all sections of the camp. Until the middle of 1941 the camp had only housed Poles, but by the end of the year other national groups had appeared and these, too, had organized their own resistance movements. After considerable difficulties, Pilecki's organization managed to unify with the most important of these, the Czechs, Russians, and later the Austrians (under the leadership of a communist, Hermann Langbein) (Langbein, 1994).

The Union of Military Organization soon became the major resistance movement at Auschwitz, but on May 1, 1943, a small group of Austrian communists and Polish socialists broke with the Union of Military Organization to form a new movement, *Kampfgruppe Auschwitz* (Auschwitz Combat Section). The *Kampfgruppe* was to be an international organization bound by working class ideology and the promise of a Soviet victory. Its leaders included the Polish socialists Jozef Cyrankiewicz (later to become Prime Minister of

Poland) and Tadeusz Holuj; the Austrian communists Hermann Langbein and Ernst Berger; and three German communists, Ludwig Worl, Karl Lill, and Bruno Baum. Ultimately a measure of solidarity was instituted, but a fully integrated movement never really appeared, severely inhibiting factors in the achievement of one of the resistance movement's basic aims, full-scale rebellion. As it turned out, none ever took place at Auschwitz.

The imminence of extermination was the trigger, however, that saw Jewish prisoners assigned to the XII *Sonderkommando* in Birkenau, on October 7, 1944, stage a rebellion in which they destroyed and severely damaged some of the crematoria, and killed a number of German guards (Müller, 1979; Venezia, 2011). When leaders of the Auschwitz underground sent an urgent warning to the tiny resistance movement in the *Sonderkommando* of the imminence of an SS action that would liquidate it, they immediately pleaded that the underground join with them launching an uprising. Such collaboration was for various reasons not forthcoming, so the members of the *Sonderkommando* decided to go ahead on their own rising. All the participants in the rebellion fell in combat. In their investigation of the affair, the Germans discovered that explosives used in the uprising had been smuggled by a group of four young Jewish women (Roza Robota, Ala Gertner, Estusia Wajcblum, and Regina Safirsztajn) elsewhere in Auschwitz. On January 6, 1945, they were publicly hanged in Auschwitz.

The rebellion was, however, an isolated incident within the camp, and did not involve the entire Auschwitz complex. Two large-scale prisoner rebellions, at Treblinka (August 2, 1943) and Sobibór (October 14, 1943) did take place, and these can be examined as cases of successful extermination camp resistance despite the odds.

Although Treblinka and Sobibór were extermination camps not designed to house large numbers of people for long periods, some prisoners were selected to act as a pool of labor for the day-to-day chores of camp life. It was these inmates who decided to organize and take on the task of breaking out of their respective camps—an undertaking that would throw the killing machinery into disarray and perhaps ensure the survival of some who would otherwise surely have been killed.

Plans at Treblinka were detailed and precise; every man had a job to do, and responsibility was delegated in such a way that each phase was dependent upon the success of that which preceded it (Arad, 1987). On August 2, 1943, after having built an arsenal consisting of hand grenades and rifles stolen from the camp armory, between 150 and 200 inmates rose in a coordinated action, rushed the fence, and attempted a breakthrough. Before this could be completed, however, the Germans became aware of the prisoners' actions, meaning that the prisoners were unable to arm themselves sufficiently to take control of the camp as they had planned. Instead, the resistance group set fire to buildings (but the gas chambers remained unscathed), and hundreds of prisoners stormed the fence surrounding the camp. Of the 700 prisoners in the camp, only about 200 made it safely into the forests nearby, where they were ruthlessly hunted down by the Nazis and by antisemitic Poles. It has been estimated that possibly fewer than forty survived the war. Killing operations then continued through August 1943. The camp was dismantled throughout that fall and winter, with the gas chambers destroyed and a farmhouse built in its place. Soviet forces entered the camp on August 16, 1944.

The revolt at Sobibór, two months later on October 14, 1943, was in many respects similar to that at Treblinka (Arad, 1987; Rashke, 2013). Largely the product of intensive military planning by Soviet troops—all Jews—interned there under the leadership of Alexander Pechersky (who had himself been in the camp for only three weeks), the revolt saw all 600 inmates make a break for freedom. Of these, about 400 actually broke out of the camp compound, though half were killed by the SS or landmines planted around the camp before they could reach the relative safety of the woods. Only about fifty survived the war. Immediately after the revolt, *Reichsführer-SS* Heinrich Himmler ordered the camp to be dismantled, and had it converted into a farm.

The timing of the closures was probably attributable to the risings, but perhaps the Nazis had already been planning to do so beforehand, as 1943 also saw the closure of two of the other death camps, Bełżec and Chełmno—where rebellions did not take place. There is little doubt that the prisoners' actions at Treblinka and Sobibór forced the Nazis' hands, however, as considerable damage was done and a great deal of reconstruction work would have been needed to bring the camps back into full operation. Yet despite the success of these two revolts, it must be stressed that rebellions on this scale were rare, and such desperate acts of coordinated violence did not exemplify resistance in the camps overall.

DISCUSSION QUESTIONS

- "Resistance was like pebbles in a stream against a raging torrent. It could never be effective." Discuss.
- What were the aims of resisters in the ghettos and extermination camps? Was there any realistic chance of them achieving those aims?
- Was there a difference in strategy, tactics, or actions between Jewish resistance and the resistance offered by non-Jewish movements?
- Were Jewish fighters in the forests resisters—or fugitives fleeing from the Holocaust?
- To what extent can upstanders who said no to the Nazis be considered as resisters?

ENDING THE HOLOCAUST

OVERVIEW

By the summer of 1944 troops from the Soviet Red Army were advancing through German-occupied territory in Eastern Europe, as the Americans and British were invading through France in the south and west. Orders went out from SS headquarters in Berlin that where the likelihood appeared that concentration camps might be captured, they would be abandoned and the prisoners in them would be evacuated and sent deeper into Germany. These forced evacuations initiated the final phase of the Holocaust, in which prisoners were sent on what became known as "death marches" (Blatman, 2011).

While some concentration camp guards left debilitated prisoners alive in their barracks, others slaughtered any too weak to walk. Those who remained behind were often locked in the camps without access to food or water; certainly, none were set free even though the SS guards or auxiliaries might have left. When the evacuations took place, some prisoners were simply ordered out on the spot, with no possibility for preparation. Others were able to grab a few items, which was some small comfort: an extra piece of clothing, a crust of bread, or a small blanket could, perhaps, increase a prisoner's chances of survival.

Most marches covered hundreds of miles, and were usually carried out with callous disregard for life. Prisoners who moved too slowly or fell out of line were immediately shot. On some marches, prisoners were murdered outright; others perished from starvation, exhaustion, or disease.

Although each death march varied in duration and destination, all prisoners experienced deprivation, debility, and the constant threat of death. Nevertheless, despite the intense distress, many prisoners shared their residual energy with others who were more vulnerable. Stories have been told by numerous survivors of acts of mutual cooperation; words of support, a shared scrap of bread, or an encouraging shoulder were gestures that could assist a fellow prisoner to last for one more day. Such camaraderie created surrogate families and also evinced a total rejection of the Nazi crusade to dehumanize their victims.

THE LIBERATION OF THE CAMPS

American author Jon Bridgman, in a key study of the liberation of the concentration camps and the end of the Holocaust, has written that the topic "has not been the subject of much scholarly attention" within studies of the topic overall (Bridgman, 1990). The essential reason for this, he has argued, is that while liberation was a dramatic moment, very little needs to be explored in depth; the Allies arrived, the SS departed, and the inmates were free. Yet there was much more to the story than that. In all camps, the liberating soldiers were shocked and angered at what they found, and genuinely troubled at the sight of the dead and near-dead who, by mid-1945, occupied the camps in their scores of thousands. The discovery of these emaciated and filthy skeletons, some alive, some not, was sickening in all senses of the word.

On June 6, 1944—D-Day—American, British, and Canadian forces invaded Europe on the coast of Normandy in Operation Overlord, starting the process that would lead to the liberation of Western Europe. In the East, the Red Army, after three years of bitter fighting, was pushing back German forces steadily, and in late July 1944 they captured the first Nazi death camp, Majdanek, in the city of Lublin. Here, in what was one of the best preserved of all the death camps, Soviet soldiers discovered the horrific machinery of the Final Solution—extermination sites outfitted with large-scale gas chambers and crematories. As 1944 unfolded the Red Army liberated or overran the sites of the other death camps, at Sobibór, Bełżec, and Treblinka. In late January 1945 Auschwitz was liberated, the Soviet soldiers rescuing the pitiful remnant that had been too sick or debilitated to be evacuated in the death marches.

In Western Europe, American and Free French forces liberated Paris in August 1944. The same month, the Allies invaded southern France in Operation Dragoon. Throughout April and May 1945, American, British, Canadian, and Free French forces liberated camps through the western half of Germany (Abzug, 1985). On April 11, the U.S. Third Army's 6th Armored Division rolled into Buchenwald, freeing 20,000 prisoners. Generals Dwight D. Eisenhower, Omar Bradley, and George S. Patton inspected many of the facilities in the surrounding towns, while starting a trend repeated throughout the occupied areas whereby local populations were forced to visit the locations of the Nazis' deeds. Later, other American forces liberated camps such as Dachau and Flossenbürg. The British Army liberated Bergen-Belsen (see p. 000) and other camps north of the American positions.

By mid-May the war was over in Europe. Once liberated, the survivors of the concentration camps faced a multitude of problems—disease, malnutrition, and the by-products of abuse from the hands of their captors. Thousands died after liberation, and tens of thousands of the living were now refugees, left with nothing and relying on the occupying Allied armies to help them reconstruct a new life. The relief and relocation process would take years to complete (see Box 7.1).

BOX 7.1 LIBERATION IN THE EAST

A ghetto was established by the Nazis at Vilna after their occupation of Lithuania on June 25, 1941, and was soon known for its brutality and high mortality rate, as starvation, disease, shootings, and deportations to concentration camps and extermination camps steadily took a terrible toll on the population. In 1943 Ida Weisbaum Feinberg, her husband Sender, and her father were deported from the ghetto to the Vaivara concentration camp, the largest Nazi camp in Estonia.

Surviving Vaivara, Ida was among those the SS began to evacuate in late August 1944 as the Soviets approached Estonia. With the Soviet offensives to re-take Estonia taking place across August and September, some 80,000 people fled the country by sea to Finland and Sweden; a further 25,000 Estonians went to Sweden, and 42,000 to Germany as it seemed as though it was only a matter of time before German forces would be pushed out of the country and Estonia would be re-occupied by the Soviet army,

Plans were made to evacuate Vaivara before it could be liberated by the Russians. While several of the departures were made by sea, with the prisoners traveling across the Baltic to Stutthof, near Danzig, other prisoners, including Ida, were subjected to death marches along the coast. The reasoning behind the evacuations was simple: the maintenance of secrecy. The Nazis, who had been practicing deception throughout the Holocaust, kept information as restricted as possible for as long as possible. In many cases they not only abandoned the camps, but also removed the remaining inmates to other locations or killed them in large numbers even before the marches commenced. As part of the secrecy at the end of the war, the Nazis showed that they were also committed to murdering as many of the victims as possible before they, themselves, were forced to lay down their arms.

During a break in the march one night, local Polish villagers approached the convoy to try to find out who they were and what they were doing there. Defying the very real prospect that they might have turned on her, Ida addressed them in Polish with the words, "I am a Jew." By way of response, some of the Poles then came to the aid of the Jewish prisoners, showing great kindness through hiding and protecting them at what would have been considerable risk. In a remarkable show of fellow-feeling, the Poles of this village provided the Jews with food, and during the daylight hours kept watch should any Germans appear.

The risks these people took were immense. Of all the countries occupied by the Nazis during World War II, it was only in Poland that help given to Jews was punishable by death. This applied not only to the rescuer but also to his or her family, a fact the German occupiers publicized widely. Under the circumstances, citizens were under no obligation to risk their lives for Jews, and even less that of their families. And yet in this circumstance, Ida and the other women in this one convoy remained safe due to the goodwill of a few Poles in a small village during the death march.

Upon being liberated by the Soviets, Ida made her way back to the vicinity of Vilna, where she was eventually reunited with her husband Sender, who had earlier, unbeknown to her, managed to escape from Vaivara (Feinberg and McLoughlin, 2008; Bartrop, 2014).

BERGEN-BELSEN: A CASE STUDY

Bergen-Belsen was situated not far from the town of Celle in northwestern Germany. It was originally designated a camp for political prisoners, and, contrary to the image many people today have of Nazi concentration camps, it was not equipped with gas chambers or crematoria. Towards the end of World War II, however, prisoners were subjected to a very limited diet, with a huge number of deaths resulting from starvation, malnutrition, or diseases like typhus and dysentery resulting from an unsanitary water supply. The guards at Bergen-Belsen were notoriously brutal, and the camp was considered an especially horrendous place to be imprisoned (Cesarani and Bargett, 2006).

In December 1944 Joseph Kramer, who the British called "The Beast of Belsen," was transferred to Bergen-Belsen from Auschwitz-Birkenau as commandant, and the regime of brutalization intensified dramatically. Beatings, torture, random shootings, and senseless cruelty became the order of the day.

Bergen-Belsen's regular prisoner muster was about 10,000. As Allied armies threatened to capture various concentration camps on the Eastern and Western fronts, prisoners were moved to camps deeper in Germany, and by April 1945 Belsen held almost 80,000 prisoners. The acute shortage of food, together with the poor water quality and next to no medical care, transformed the camp into a crisis site of catastrophic proportions, and Kramer lost control of the situation. The guards stopped keeping track of prisoners, refraining from contact because they were afraid of catching typhus. Any semblance of order simply disappeared.

British troops captured Bergen-Belsen in April 1945. Upon touring the camp, they found some 30,000 starving and diseased survivors, with 35,000 corpses lying in various parts of the camp. Film footage from the time became an iconic testament to the brutality of the Nazi regime. Kramer, for his part, was sentenced to death by a British military court on November 17, 1945, and hanged a few days later.

Bergen-Belsen was perhaps the supreme example of the chaos, overcrowding and general horror that struck all the camps. With an inmate population that had grown fourfold in two months, the area was a charnel house when the British arrived, and they set the captured Nazi guards to work helping gather the dead together in advance of their burial. Most of those who had died were simply piled up in what became mountains of putrescent flesh, which were then shoved unceremoniously into giant pits dug by British Army bulldozers (Shephard, 2006).

Rabbi Leslie Hardman, a British Military Chaplain, came to Bergen-Belsen the day after its liberation. When he arrived, what he saw beggared all description. In his memoir, he attempted to convey something of what he encountered in the camp. We read his incredulity, for example, at seeing those still alive, who, he writes, were "a tottering mass of blackened skin and bones, held together somehow with filthy rags." As for the vast number of dead, his immediate feeling was that they were asleep; he had no idea that so many could be dead in such a concentrated space. With such carnage, he felt overwhelmed: "a pygmy grappling with a mountain" (Hardman, 1958).

The challenges he would face over succeeding weeks would be enough to make him question everything he had thought was "normal" up to this time. As he drove into the camp on April 16, 1945, he realized that the dead needed to be buried as a matter of urgency. A large bulldozer was at work; it had already eaten out a pit large enough to hold 5,000 bodies. It then began to push into the mound of corpses, shoving the bodies into the hole it had made. Aghast, Rabbi Harman begged the officer in charge to show some reverence for the dead. The response shocked him: the bodies had to be buried as quickly as possible in order to reduce the danger of disease. Rabbi Hardman was advised to come back later (Hardman, 1958).

Evacuation of the camp began on April 21, 1945. As each of the barracks was cleared, they were burned down to combat the spread of typhus. On May 19, evacuation was completed and two days later the ceremonial burning of the last barracks brought to an end the first stage of relief operations. As many people as could be mustered were brought to a makeshift assembly ground and watched the destruction of that last barrack block, with British troops using flamethrowers to ceremonially burn it down.

What remained of Belsen was then converted into a Displaced Persons' (DP) camp, eventually to serve as the largest DP camp in Europe, holding more than 12,000 Jews. It became the only exclusively Jewish camp in the British zone of Germany. Within the camp, some form of regular life resumed; a camp committee was established, and political, cultural, and religious activities were organized. Jewish family life was renewed, and during the first few months an average of twenty marriages were performed each day; more than 2,000 children were born to survivors (Flanagan and Bloxham, 2005).

Today, nothing remains of the camp itself. What is left is a graveyard; most of the graves are unmarked, and several of those with gravestones say only, "Here lies an unknown deceased." A documentation center and museum can now also be visited at the site.

AFTER LIBERATION: THE DISPLACED PERSONS' CAMPS

By 1947, perhaps up to 8 million (and possibly more) people found themselves displaced from their homes throughout Europe, including over 250,000 Jews, most of whom had been released from the various Nazi concentration, labor, and extermination camps.

Many of these people, now free, fled westward, fearful of finding themselves in the Soviet zone of occupation and subject to repatriation (or worse). For those who either had no homes or towns to which they could return, or wished to return, or no countries prepared to accept their return, major dilemmas arose over how they were to be housed, clothed, fed, and provided with medical services. These became a nightmare for the occupying Allies. To ease the urgency, camps of convenience—Displaced Persons' camps—were created for these people in Germany, Austria, Italy, and some other countries formerly occupied by the Nazis (Wyman, 1998).

At their maximum, approximately 850,000 people, from an array of backgrounds, were housed in these camps. The plight of the Jewish refugees, however, was somewhat unique: all too often they found themselves in camps alongside of avowed antisemites, a situation manifesting itself in some instances as violence. Ultimately, in many situations, this necessitated their segregation into separate camps.

This division came after United States President Harry S. Truman had read a report from University of Pennsylvania Law School Dean Earl G. Harrison, who visited the camps between July and August 1945 and found the situation there intolerable. With regard to the situation prevailing for the Jews, he wrote that many were "living under guard behind barbed-wire fences" and "had no clothing other than their concentration camp garb." The environments were sub-standard, with many of the buildings "clearly unfit for winter." Speaking of the Allied administrations, Harrison noted that

> We appear to be treating the Jews as the Nazis treated them except that we do not exterminate them. They are in concentration camps in large numbers under our military guard instead of SS troops. One is led to wonder whether the German people, seeing this, are not supposing that we are following or at least condoning Nazi policy.
>
> (Stevens, 1956)

Harrison was equally critical of the military administration of Supreme Allied Commander General Dwight D. Eisenhower, and tension developed between the two as Eisenhower attempted to explain and rationalize to Truman the reality of the conditions. Of necessity, as Eisenhower understood it, the Allies found themselves having to make use of whatever facilities were presented: military barracks, hotels, hospitals, castles, and even private homes. Camp conditions ranged from deplorable, to harsh, to livable. Sometimes foodstuffs were rationed; sometimes there was enough to feed all. Curfews were imposed, particularly in the early days, and the DPs were forbidden to interact with local townspeople.

Relatively quickly, once camp life assumed a reasonable measure of stability and routine, the residents themselves were hard at work, establishing synagogues and churches, newspapers, and cultural and educational endeavors. They were aided in these efforts by various international humanitarian organizations and agencies, including the American Jewish Joint Distribution Committee; American Friends Service Committee ("the Quakers") and their British counterpart the British Friends Relief Service; Catholic charities; the International Committee of the Red Cross; the International Lutheran World Federation; and many other national and international organizations. Those DPs (by far the majority of whom were not Jewish) who could emigrate did so as well, for the most part to countries outside of Europe. By 1953, however, more than 250,000 refugees still remained throughout Europe with no place to go.

Jewish refugees, however, remained with a distinct set of problems and difficulties. Referring to themselves as the *Sh'erit ha-Pletah* ("The Saving Remnant"), the overwhelming majority did not wish to remain in Europe, but preferred to emigrate—primarily to the British Mandate of Palestine. The difficulty here was that the British denied Jewish admission so as not to offend the Arab population, though for Zionists entry to Palestine remained a primary objective. Between 1945 and 1948, therefore, illegal immigration became the only option, and an underground organized effort known as *Bricha* (escape) accounted for more than 100,000 to 150,000 Jews being smuggled into Palestine prior to the creation of Israel in May 1948 (Bauer, 1970).

On October 1, 1945, the United Nations Relief and Rehabilitation Administration, which had already begun directing such camp efforts, now took responsibility for easing the lot of the DPs, while still relying on the military for transportation, security, and supply-lines. By the end of the year, more than 6,000,000 refugees throughout Europe had been repatriated. These did not include so-called "ethnic Germans," between 12 million and

14 million of whom had been expelled from Eastern and Central Europe by 1950, when all but two of the DP camps had been closed—Föhrenwald in 1957 and Wels in 1959.

The DP camps were an immediate necessity in the aftermath of the chaotic days following Germany's defeat and the end of war, coupled with both the devastation existing throughout Europe and the tensions already beginning to surface between the countries of the West and the Soviet Union. Successful efforts at meeting refugee needs were coupled with limited repatriation efforts and failures, all of which were heightened by the specific plight of the Jews.

THE NUREMBERG TRIALS

On November 20, 1945, the trial of major Nazi war criminals at Nuremberg began, its fundamental intention being to punish those members of Germany's Nazi government and High Command for having led the world into war and perpetrating innumerable horrors against those caught in the Nazi net. A secondary ambition was to set in place a legal precedent for dealing with any future violations of the world's peace, a peace the new United Nations organization was committed to upholding. The trial was to be the first in history for crimes committed against the peace of the world (Conot, 1983).

The basis of the trials was laid out on August 8, 1945, when the United States, the Soviet Union, Britain, and France signed the London Charter after a conference determined what charges would be brought against the captured Nazi leaders now that the war had ended.

When the International Military Tribunal (IMT), based in the German city of Nuremberg, sat for the purpose of trying twenty-two major Nazis in November 1945, the accused were charged under any of four counts:

- "The Common Plan," that is, taking part in conspiracy to commit Crimes against Peace, War Crimes, and Crimes against Humanity;
- Crimes against Peace, that is, participating in the planning and waging of wars of aggression in violation of international treaties and agreements;

- War Crimes, that is, murder and ill-treatment of civilians in occupied territory or on the high seas, deportations for slave labor, murder or ill-treatment of war prisoners, killing of hostages, plunder, exacting collective penalties, wanton destruction and devastation, conscription of civilian labor, forcing civilians to swear allegiance to a hostile Power, and Germanization of occupied territories; and Crimes against Humanity, that is, murder, extermination, enslavement, deportation, other inhumane acts committed against civilian populations before the war and during the war, and persecution on political, religious, and racial grounds in the Common Plan mentioned in count 1.

These trials were to set the tone for all subsequent war crimes trials down to the present day (Conot, 1983; Persico, 1994).

The major emphasis of the IMT lay in a concern to bring to justice those who had upset the international order by waging aggressive war, not those who had exclusively committed egregious acts of barbarity. Ever since Nuremberg, however—and with an increasing tempo—an impression has developed that the trials had, as their major focus, something to do with the Holocaust and the other atrocities committed by the Nazis. Indeed, while these events did in fact form a major part of the indictments, and were specifically covered in count 4 (Crimes against Humanity), it is important to record that the IMT was not established in order to punish the leaders of the Third Reich for the Holocaust.

On the contrary, the main intention of Nuremberg was to try those who were held to have been responsible for bringing about the war, and to hold them accountable for the damage and loss of life that had been caused as a result of it.

Because of the shocking nature of the revelations made about atrocities committed against Jews, however, from an early date Nuremberg came to be seen first and foremost as a Tribunal judging the anti-human evils perpetrated by the Third Reich. The indictment relating to Crimes against Humanity rapidly became the count which most clearly represented the abhorrence held by people around the world at what they understood Nazism to mean.

It is worthwhile considering, for a moment, the four indictments. The first, "The Common Plan," was in reality a general indictment summarizing the other three, and charged the accused with engaging in a conspiracy to commit them. The second, Crimes against Peace, charged the accused with causing the war that had just been fought. Only in counts 3 and 4 (War Crimes and Crimes against Humanity, respectively) was the human dimension to the Nazis' wrongdoing introduced. Graphic though they are, the issues specified in counts 3 and 4 were secondary to the Tribunal's primary aim; namely, the punishment of those found guilty for the planning and waging of aggressive war as stipulated in count 2.

Nuremberg should thus be seen as more than a trial sitting in judgment on the Holocaust. Nothing was seen in the first instance as being more criminal that the foisting of aggressive war upon a world which had previously been clearly committed to avoiding it. Yet the alignment of Jewish horrors with the IMT was more and more apparent as each new day dawned. News of Nazi atrocities was broadcast all over the world, and rapidly became the central motif justifying Nuremberg. Its main effect would see the Tribunal as a trial for the Holocaust, with the main reason—the planning and waging of aggressive war—falling by the wayside.

When the IMT (comprised of two judges each from Britain, France, the United States, and the Soviet Union) handed down its decisions, six of the accused were found guilty on all four counts, and sentenced to hang; another six were similarly sentenced after having been found guilty on some of the counts. Others received long prison sentences ranging from ten years to life, while three were acquitted and (after some delay) released (Persico, 1994).

There was no doubt that Nuremberg resulted in landmark judgments. Never before had such an international tribunal of victor nations sat to deliver verdicts over a vanquished foe, and never before had there been such a vast set of compromises made across often competing legal systems in order to reach a convergence of opinion. In the aftermath of the IMT, another twelve separate trials took place, also at Nuremberg, between 1946 and 1949. These considered the fates of the SS as a criminal organization, Nazi physicians who had conducted medical experiments against prisoners, *Kommandants* of Nazi concentration camps, leaders of major business enterprises, and the like. One hundred and seventy-seven persons were convicted and sentenced either to death or terms of imprisonment.

While the Holocaust itself was not on trial, nonetheless the revelations that came as a result served to confirm for people living in the Allied countries why the struggle against the Nazis had been too important to lose.

THE "CRIME WITHOUT A NAME" GETS ITS NAME

On August 24, 1941, British Prime Minister Winston Churchill delivered a live broadcast from London, in which he described the barbarity of the German occupation in Russia. His speech was made just over two months after the Nazi invasion of the Soviet Union in Operation Barbarossa, and the introduction of brutally repressive measures against the civilian population.

Among his comments was the statement that the Nazis were instituting "frightful cruelties," in which "whole districts are being exterminated." He identified that "Scores of thousands ... of executions in cold blood are being perpetrated by the German Police-troops," and that never since "the Mongol invasions of Europe in the sixteenth century" had there been "methodical, merciless butchery" on or approaching such a scale. Further, he said, "this is but the beginning," as famine and pestilence would be likely to follow. In short, he concluded, "We are in the presence of a crime without a name" (Gilbert, 2007a: 186).

What Churchill could not say, at the time, was that the world was witnessing genocide. The term itself was yet to be coined; this would only happen when introduced by Raphael Lemkin in 1944, in a book he published in the United States entitled *Axis Rule in Occupied Europe: Laws of Occupation, Analysis of Government, Proposals for Redress* (Lemkin, 1944). With this, Lemkin gave a name to the crime identified by Churchill: genocide, which he referred to as a "new term and new conception for destruction of nations." With the end of the war and the Holocaust, Lemkin became obsessed with the cause of seeking recognition for his term from the newly established United Nations, and achieving passage of a bill banning such destruction in international law. He faced considerable difficulties, not the least of which was that he was just one man with a theory, acting in no official capacity or representing any agency or government.

After many bureaucratic and legal battles, on December 9, 1948, the General Assembly of the United Nations, with the support of both its Legal Committee and the Security Council, passed the Convention for the Prevention and Punishment of the Crime of Genocide. The vote was unanimous, and the struggle against massive human rights violations, in light of the Holocaust, entered a new era.

DISCUSSION QUESTIONS

- Did the evacuation of concentration and extermination camps in the East serve as an indication that liberation was approaching?
- Could it be argued that the conditions surrounding the death marches in 1944 and 1945 were an extension of those in the concentration camps from which the prisoners were leaving?
- What was the response of the Allied armies as they liberated the various camps? Did these responses vary? Why?
- What evidence did the liberators uncover concerning the reality of the Holocaust during 1944 and 1945?
- What were some responses by prisoners to their newly liberated state once they were freed?

SURVIVORS REFLECT ON THE HOLOCAUST

OVERVIEW

Considering the experience of the end of the Holocaust—and what it signified for those who survived—it is appropriate to look at the words of those who lived through it, as a pathway to understanding.

A Hungarian Jew, S.B. Unsdorfer, had been in an outside work party at Buchenwald. It was wound up on April 10, 1945, and the prisoners were force-marched back to the main camp. Examining his feelings during the march, Unsdorfer reflected that what lay ahead "was going to be the Battle of Life"; with the Allies closing in as the column raced towards Buchenwald, he realized that

> [l]ife, freedom, and liberation were pursuing us. Death, destruction and suffering were facing us. All that had happened since my family and I had been driven into [the ghetto at] Sered was about to be resolved. The Hour was surely coming nearer. Whose would it be?
>
> (Unsdorfer, 1961)

The question was to be answered a few days later, after the column had reached Buchenwald main camp. The prisoners were told that they were to be transferred, on foot, to Dachau, far away to the south:

> "Dachau?" we echoed in surprise. "But that's about five hundred kilometers away. How can anyone survive it?"
> "You can't," they said, their gaunt faces emotionless.

> And indeed, the awful news trickled through to us that about one in three or four hundred was expected to survive this dreadful march; the rest would die on the roads from starvation, exhaustion, or bullets.
>
> (Unsdorfer, 1961)

Marching prisoners crisscrossed Europe during the last days of the war, and most accounts relate stories of horror, further degradation, and sudden death. For the vast majority of accounts written by former Auschwitz inmates, moreover, the evacuations were compounded by the bitterness of a particularly harsh Polish winter.

A Norwegian woman who had been incarcerated at Auschwitz, Sylvia Salvesen, has left a graphic testimony of her evacuation to Ravensbrück:

> The camp of Auschwitz was evacuated on January 15th, 1945. All had to go. Thousands of prisoners were driven along the snow-covered roads by German SS soldiers. There were no doctors, no nurses, no medicine. Those who could not walk were shot. The prisoners walked for three and a half days. Many froze to death, or had their hands and feet frostbitten. Many died from exhaustion. When the transport finally arrived at Ravensbrück they had to stand for a day and a half in a street behind the camp Hospital. There was no room for them in the blocks. The camp was overfull already.
>
> (Salvesen, 1958)

For Halina Birenbaum, another prisoner on the same march, "all awareness of reality" began to fade, as "the frost, sleepiness and weakness acted like a narcotic" (Birenbaum, 1971). As the ordeal lengthened, she observed that sustenance became a greater problem than it had been even in the camp:

> They drove us on, continually promising a halt, a rest. Another mile, they said—a few more steps. We had nothing to eat or drink but snow. The frost increased, the road became as smooth and slippery as glass, acrobatic feats were necessary so as not to twist one's ankle, especially in my hobnailed boots. At one point, my supplies of energy gave out, so

did my capacity for controlling my muscles. I felt I could not take another step.

(Birenbaum, 1971)

Halina did manage to keep going, as did many others, through a burning desire to stay alive, to see this experience through to the end, to outlive the Nazi regime. This was an experience offering no respite. In the camp, there had often been ways to place one prisoner in a slightly better position than another, even temporarily. But on the death marches, all were as one.

For Heda Margolius, a young Jewish woman from Czechoslovakia, there was something comforting in this common suffering: "Shuffling along together we had a sense of belonging, the knowledge that we were all equally frozen, starved, and abused. We had a common fate, a common road underfoot and somewhere along that road even a common death" (Margolis, 1973).

The despair the Nazis had tried so hard to instill in the camps drove many prisoners to give up, but for others the idea that they were at last out from behind the barbed wire was sufficient to rekindle thoughts of liberation. Heda Margolius recalled:

> if we broke free ... and then it would dawn on me: at this moment it would take no more than a single act, a single decision, to win the greatest freedom one could have in our age, in our corner of the world. As soon as I slipped out from under the bayonets, I would be standing outside the entire system. I might win only a few days, more likely a few hours, but it would be a freedom millions didn't even dream about. I would belong nowhere, I would belong to nothing. No one would know I existed, all the rules and prohibitions would no longer apply to me. I would be outside, outside of it all. When they caught me, I would be like a wind trapped in a sail, a bird shot in flight.
>
> (Margolius, 1973)

The ugliness of death was ever-present, right through to the arrival of liberating Allied troops. But for many prisoners there was a burning desire to keep going—to defeat the Nazis by staying alive until liberation, although there were no consistent motives underlying the will to survive. For some, it was based on a spirit of revenge; for others, there was desperation for reunion with lost family members, a desire to bear witness, a spiritual quest for the ideal of freedom itself, or a religious commitment to live in order to serve God. Once the camps had been freed, prisoners had to face up to what their new status would entail, and after having dreamed about their liberation for so long, some wondered whether it was really all a bit of an anti-climax.

When prisoners from the Nazi concentration camps were freed in 1945, their emotions were diverse. Several themes can be discerned, from which a number of expressions related by survivors become apparent. About the only credible reality to be faced was an ugly death, a sudden, unavoidable fact which was ultimately intended to be everyone's lot. At Belsen in January 1945, one prisoner reflected that "there was no dignity left in dying" (Pawlowicz, 1964); elsewhere, death "was the natural thing" (d'Harcourt, 1967), an occurrence that "meant salvation" (Weiss, 1961) for those whom it visited.

THE URGE TO SURVIVE

Many prisoners felt that death would pass them by. At the end of the first day of a death march, for example, when the full reality of their situation hit them, the fatalism of some prisoners became even further entrenched, but this was tempered by an unquenchable optimism and thirst for life:

> Even then, after that horrific first day's march, no one really believed this was a diabolical plan completely to exterminate us. We fondly imagined that the weak and sick would fall by the way and that the strong would find themselves in a new camp. No thought was given to the identity of those who had perished. What did it matter, provided one was alive oneself?
>
> (Weiss, 1961)

Others even rejected the possibility of death, and allowed themselves to be deluded by the Nazis' stories of a positive future life. As Halina Birenbaum recorded later, "I preferred any lie a thousand times, as long as it gave me the hope of surviving" (Birenbaum, 1971).

Neither life nor death was predictable. The experience of living through (and surviving) the Holocaust was bearable or unbearable, death-ridden or life-affirming, depending on each person's own individual perspective. Where one prisoner might state that "to understand our daily calvary you have to imagine a human condition in which *every* moment is unbearable" (Lewinska, 1968), another could acknowledge that "life was unbearable, yet it was borne," as "there was still a spark of desperate hope of which we were not consciously aware" (Weiss, 1961).

However one perceived the ongoing daily torment, each morning brought a new day, and every evening saw that day's survival. Seweryna Szmaglewska, a Polish prisoner in Birkenau in 1942, saw it this way:

> There are certain matters which the mind slips hurriedly over, in the same way that the feet avoid the sick and dead lying on the ground. There are so many things you must take care of to make the next day in the field more bearable. At the moment you enter the gate when the sun sets, your mind begins detailed plans of things to do that night, creating a bridge over reality. You live only for each day. On this purposeless pilgrimage you walk like a blind man groping from object to object, from morning to evening, putting all your energy into the maintenance of life throughout the day.
>
> (Szmaglewska, 1947)

And at the end of that day? Yuri Pilyar, a Soviet prisoner of war, reflected on this after a day's grueling labor:

> Tomorrow—June the 23rd, 1943—our nightmare would begin anew, but in the meantime I could strike some kind of balance. We had not been shot, but we were still condemned men, that was obvious. We were all earmarked for the crematorium, but that need not necessarily happen very soon. ... What mattered was that we were alive, alive! I could look up at the sky, breathe freely and even enjoy a minute's rest. And that was not little!
>
> (Pilyar, 1960)

Reflections of this kind, often glimpsed in a brief moment of respite, gave concentration camp prisoners the hope needed to keep going when all seemed lost. The more they communicated their ideas to others, the better it was for all concerned. Optimism, no less than hopelessness, could be infectious.

This spirit of going on regardless of their trials sometimes led certain inmates to speculate as to why it should have been so. After all, the forces working on the prisoners to give up were substantial, exaggerated in the concentration camp to a vastly greater degree than outside.

Elie Aron Cohen, for example, a Dutch Jewish doctor in Auschwitz, became aware in the camp that his wife and son had been killed. His intense grief was accompanied by an astonishment that hearing this news only served to help him go on fighting:

> There will undoubtedly have been those who didn't, once they knew. But I did. Nor did I see any others giving in. Everyone went on fighting again. ... That will to live, that forcing yourself to carry on, that survives. It just happens like that. Of course, you got into a state of shock, and the shock was bigger for one man than for another ... oh, well, I don't know, and I can't really explain it very clearly. I wanted to go on living. It isn't a noble attitude maybe. But it's true. That's how it is.
>
> (Cohen, 1973)

For others, as recalled by S.B. Unsdorfer, the accent was on simply "hang[ing] on to dear life by trying to find hope and courage beyond human power" (Unsdorfer, 1961).

SURVIVAL AND LUCK

All this notwithstanding, it must never be forgotten that once inside a camp the life of every Jew (and most other inmates) was surrendered to the Nazis, who could do with the prisoners what they wished, even unto death. An inmate from Dachau put the issue succinctly: "The concentration camps were only a macabre lottery. Those who held the lucky numbers were bound to get out. The others, of course, all lost" (Gun, 1966). In her interviews with Holocaust survivors living in the United States after the war, Dorothy Rabinowitz spoke to a survivor who articulated most thoroughly the notion of chance:

> being spared was a matter of luck; she said it often. Smarter people than herself had tried to figure out ways to stay alive; they had devoted themselves day and night to the task of planning how they could survive this way and that—brilliant people they had been, some of them—and they had been killed anyway. It was luck, because if you thought a thousand years, you could not have planned your way out of the situations she had been in; no planning could have devised the steps that impulse and accident had provided to save her. ... In addition, the more experience one had of being saved, the more one believed in the possibility of being saved; the more one saw of one's own good fortune, the less accidental it appeared; it began to seem bound, somehow, to the way in which one's life was supposed to go.
>
> (Rabinowitz, 1976)

Germaine Tillion, a Frenchwoman imprisoned at Ravensbrück, addressed the issue further when summing up why she lived on after the Nazis had left:

> The fact that I survived Ravensbrück I owe first—and most definitely—to chance, then to anger and the motivation to reveal the crimes I had witnessed, and finally to a union of friendship, since I had lost the instinctive and physical desire to live.
>
> (Tillion, 1975)

For Germaine, survival required the intersection of a number of strands, of which chance was but one.

FREEDOM

And what, in the prisoners' minds, was the freedom for which they yearned? Seweryna Szmaglewska, who was sent to Birkenau in 1942 and remained there until liberated by the Russians in January 1945, wrote about it this way:

> "Freedom" is some kind of country or planet unbelievably beautiful, where every prisoner lived for a time. They tell each other about it. They reminisce. In the long sleepless hours they dream of each happening that took place, they relive it intensely, they conduct imaginary conversations with people who remained on that planet. They beg those folks to wait for their return. They cultivate that lost land in their hearts.
>
> (Szmaglewska, 1947)

Some prisoners longed for the arrival of freedom simply in order to be able to show that victory over the camp system had been achieved; seen in this light, evacuation and a death march seemed a cruel joke played by fate. Gisella Perl, a Jewish doctor from Hungary imprisoned in the women's camp at Auschwitz, expressed her thoughts in the face of the Soviet advance and her consequent transfer to another camp:

> This was not how I imagined it! During the interminable months, waiting for the day of liberation, I had seen myself again and again, leading my fellow-sufferers to freedom. I had seen myself walking ahead of them, laughing, singing songs of freedom, a human being going to meet other human beings with gratitude and dignity, to thank them for our liberation.
>
> (Perl, 1948)

That this was not the way she left Auschwitz was a source of deep anguish. To be able to leave the camp under one's own power was considered a victory, as so many others had left by the only other means possible: "as smoke *via* the chimney of the gas chamber" (Cohen, 1973). Little wonder that for many prisoners the fact that they emerged alive from the camps was a cause to be "happy, simply happy" (Cohen, 1973).

REVENGE

For others, however, the idea of liberation—whether imagined or real—had an altogether different meaning. Freedom could bring the opportunity to exact revenge on those who brought the inmates into their current condition, to reassert their humanity by reducing that of the Nazis. Hence, prisoners could argue that "Before I die one of them must" (Zywulska, 1951), or that the one ambition remaining was to become a guard over the Nazis—not for long, "just a year or so" (Berger, 1962). As if to underscore the point that this was not simple chatter but serious talk of retribution, the words of a woman working close to the Auschwitz *Sonderkommando*, servicing the gas chambers and crematoria, will suffice: "I don't want to live for the sake of living. I have no one. They gassed my whole family. I just want revenge" (Zywulska, 1951).

How typical such thoughts were for all prisoners is hard to tell, though we may be reasonably sure that every inmate at one time or another felt resentment and frustration build to a point where notions of revenge at least crossed their mind. For some, these feelings spilled over into concrete action; for others, traditional forms of coping, such as postponement or transferal of anger in another direction, were employed.

RELIGIOUS BELIEF

One area thus far untouched is that of religion. In the blackness of the camps, where death ruled and the Nazis' intention was that all moral values would be turned upside down, did religion play any role in sustaining the inmates? To what degree, moreover, did they even think about such things? While an entire library has been created considering questions of theodicy in light of the Holocaust, relatively little work has been done examining just how the prisoners themselves viewed questions of religion *whilst they were incarcerated*.

Few, for example, record prayer or religious faith as the motive force aiding their survival. While some Jews and Christians certainly prayed and engaged in religious rituals whenever they could, relatively few have left accounts in which they say they did so. Most accounts dealing with the issue at all do so through denying the existence of God in the camps, rather than affirming a divine presence or conceding that religion played any part in their survival. What might have been said later is not necessarily the same as what was felt by inmates in the camps at the time.

Take, for example, Elizabeth K., a survivor being interviewed by Dorothy Rabinowitz in the United States several decades after the war:

> do not mistake me, I am not an unbeliever. I always had faith in a Superpower. But not a Jewish God. If there was one, how could this have happened? You see, I cannot get it through my head that God would try to punish six million Jews. A Superpower, yes, without that I could not have survived.
>
> (Rabinowitz, 1976)

Likewise, Elie Wiesel, in Auschwitz, did not at first deny God's existence—only "His absolute justice." Elsewhere, he "felt revolt rise up in me. Why should I bless His name? The Eternal, Lord of the Universe, the All-Powerful and Terrible, was silent. What had I to thank Him for?" (Wiesel, 1976)

Early in 1945, as the Nazis launched a starvation campaign against the prisoners at the Buchenwald sub-camp of Neustadt, Halina Birenbaum

> deliberately and with relish declared revenge on that God who had been believed in at the home of my parents, but who had deserted us all in our misery and who, here in the Nazi concentration camps, had proved to be an invention of fraudulent priests who ordered us to love and respect Him, and fear His justice!
>
> (Birenbaum, 1971)

Another youngster, in Theresiestadt, confided to his sister:

> I cannot believe in God. If there is a God, it is the chemical in your cells. The stuff that holds life together. And sometimes, like when you are hungry or something hurts you very much—imagine I take a knife and—well, there is nothing left inside you. God leaks out. The cells break. Just pain or hunger is left and no space for God.
>
> (Berger, 1962)

As a final lamentation at God's impotence, Odd Nansen, an inmate of the notorious Grini prison in Norway, confided to his diary in April 1942:

> If there were a god [sic], he would be bound to stop this now, at least if he is all they make him out to be: the God of justice, the God of goodness, the God of love. How false and hollow it all sounds today, on this background! Who can speak today of the God of love, the God of justice? Only Germans.
>
> (Nansen, 1949)

While examples such as these would seem to indicate that concentration camp prisoners repudiated belief in God (or rather, saw that God had forsaken *them*), the question must be asked as to how representative they are of the broader situation prevailing across the entire camp universe. Did *all* such prisoners feel the same way as those quoted here? The answer must clearly be no, but the occasions on which we see survivor accounts declaiming God, and decrying religion in general, point to the fact that many inmates who had once adhered to religion in some form or another now no longer did so. At the very least, their faith underwent a negative transformation, even if it did not manifest itself as outright denial (Brenner, 1980).

THE HUMAN CONDITION

Possibly because of these thoughts, many prisoners had, of necessity, to focus on the here and now. What, therefore, did incarceration in the camps tell them about the human condition? A great many prisoners have reflected on this in their accounts, and a general consensus could be summed up in the words of David Rousset, a French political prisoner liberated by the Americans in 1945:

> It is still far too soon to draw up the positive balance sheet of concentration camp experience, but, even now, it promises to be a rich one. A dynamic awareness of the strength and beauty of being alive, self-contained, brutal, entirely stripped of all superstructures, of being able to live even in the midst

of the most appalling catastrophes or the most serious setbacks. A fresh sensual feeling of joy, arising out of the most scientific knowledge of destruction and, as a result of this, an increased firmness in action and unshakeable judgements; in short, a fuller and more intensely creative state of being. ... For some, it has been a confirmation, for most, a discovery, and a striking one.

(Rousset, 1951)

Looking at survival as an act of revelation might not have occupied every prisoner's thoughts, but many survivors have since expressed themselves along similar lines. Hence, British prisoner Christopher Burney found that in Buchenwald "one found one's fellow-men stripped of the frills and furbelows of their conditions and saw their true worth and their true feelings as human beings" (Burney, 1945).

Eugene Heimler, a Hungarian Jew who had been deported to Auschwitz in early July 1944, discussed this issue of human character with his comrades in the camp. One of them, a certain Dr. Eckstein, conveyed his opinion with the following:

[W]hat do you think determines the destiny of a person? What does it depend on, whether one is dragged down by suffering, or raised to a higher level by it? What decides our fundamental sensitivity or insensibility? Bio-chemists attribute it all to the hormones; psychologists to early and unresolved conflicts, sociologists put everything down to poverty and unsatisfactory working conditions. Have a look around. How many of these people did you know back home? Quite a number. Of the good ones, how many have remained good? And how many of them who used to be bad have become human beings here? The concentration camps have created a civilisation within a civilisation. And in this new civilisation the truths and laws whose validity we have believed in for centuries have been turned upside down.

(Heimler, 1961)

Jorge Semprun, a Spaniard arrested in France as a political opponent of the Nazis, saw the issue this way:

in the camps man ... becomes that invincible being capable of sharing his last cigarette butt, his last piece of bread, his last breath, to sustain his fellow man. That is, man doesn't become that invincible animal in the camps. He already is.

(Semprun, 1963)

Others would agree with him, not least the aforementioned Dr. Eckstein in conversation with Eugene Heimler. He described two kinds of person emerging from the camps: one, a selfish individual who will turn against society; the other, a person who will be

more humane than ever before. He will have learnt something that no other form of education could have taught him. He will have learnt the value of life, his own and that of others, and the worth of freedom, too. These, who will throw in the last atom of strength on the side of justice and truth, will become the martyrs of tomorrow and possibly also its saints.

(Heimler, 1961)

For the survivors, questions as to the nature of revealed truth, the presence or absence of God, the quality of evil and suffering, and all the words needed to answer them, are meaningless without recalling the human dimensions of the concentration camp experience. In this sense we could agree with Jorge Semprun who, as a survivor, stated that "we didn't need the camps to understand that man is a being capable of the most noble as well as the basest acts" (Semprun, 1963). For the survivors, the camps were not a modern-day version of the story of Job; their survival was not for the sole purpose of revealing some higher level of understanding of what it is to be human.

DISCUSSION QUESTIONS

- Given all they went through, do Holocaust survivors view their overall experience in the Holocaust in a positive or negative light?
- Was the Holocaust a tragedy for the Jews, for the Germans, or for both? Why?

- Are there any "lessons" that can be learned from the Holocaust?
- Was the Holocaust a watershed event in world history? Why?
- Can the Holocaust be viewed in any ways other than historically? What are they?

CONCLUSION
Holocaust Memory and the Future

OVERVIEW

For those generations coming after World War II, its memory has produced powerful responses. The legacies of the Holocaust, as will be seen, are most frequently manifested through memorials, museums, and in popular culture (especially literature and movies), but there are also other ways in which the Holocaust is recalled for those of us living in today's world.

In many places around the world, for instance, education about the Holocaust is mandatory in high school curricula, while elsewhere individual teachers or school boards seek to increase offerings on the Holocaust as electives. Universities on all continents offer undergraduate and graduate courses on the Holocaust, often taught by outstanding teachers who are among the key thinkers shaping the field.

Through education and a free exchange of ideas, scholars and others from around the world have sought to find ways to enhance understanding about the Holocaust or at least create a climate in which options are canvassed. Starting with considerations about the Holocaust but broadening out to encompass other examples of genocide, the International Association of Genocide Scholars (IAGS), for example, is a global, interdisciplinary, non-partisan organization that aims to further research and teaching about the nature, causes, and consequences of genocide, and to advance policy studies on genocide prevention. Founded in 1994, the Association meets biennially in a conference format to consider comparative research, new directions in scholarship, case studies, the links between genocide and massive human rights violations, and prevention and punishment of genocide. Since being established, several important academic conferences have taken place, the aim being to focus intensively on questions of genocide, and to draw colleagues from different disciplines into an interdisciplinary conversation. Membership of the IAGS is open to scholars, graduate students, and other interested persons worldwide (www.genocidescholarsorg/).

In like manner, the International Network of Genocide Scholars is also dedicated to genocide prevention. Established in January 2005 at an inaugural meeting in Berlin, Germany, its express purpose is to provide genocide studies with a non-partisan community in which to research and present analysis on any aspect of genocide studies, fostering scholarly exchange between individuals and institutions worldwide. Membership is open to researchers from all academic disciplines working on genocide and mass violence from within and outside Europe (https://inogs.com/).

Within the United Kingdom, the British Association for Holocaust Studies brings together academics, teachers, and other educators in an effort to further knowledge and teaching about the Holocaust. It provides a forum for academic discussion and the exchange of ideas, advertising of conferences and calls for papers, collating current research projects, and the submission of articles for consideration by its publication, *Holocaust Studies: A Journal of Culture and History* (http://britishholocauststudies.blogspot.com/).

The moral challenges posed by the Holocaust were at once immense, profound, and deeply challenging. This was no more so than in the area of religious belief and observance. It exposed the most fundamental questions of theodicy—if God is all loving and all powerful, why do the righteous suffer and wicked prosper? Did God break the Covenant with the Jewish people at Auschwitz? Where was God/Christ/Man in the shadow of the death camps?

A vast scholarly literature has been generated since the 1950s, with both Jewish and Christian theologians discussing and debating a plethora of issues arising from just such concerns (Rubenstein and Roth, 2003). In addition, while Jewish liturgy has not undergone any fundamental changes as a result of the Holocaust (though a - memorial day, Yom Hashoah, was introduced by the State of Israel in 1951, and passed into law in 1959), the shock of the Holocaust led to a fundamental transformation of one of the tenets of Roman Catholic doctrine regarding the culpability of the Jews in the Crucifixion of Christ, as expressed in *Nostra Aetate*, a declaration promulgated on October 28, 1965, by Pope Paul VI as a result of the Second Vatican Council (Connelly, 2012).

Another area of legacy to the Holocaust is to be found in the establishment of the State of Israel as the national home for the Jewish people forecast in the Balfour Declaration of November 1917. Discussions have varied as to whether or not the Holocaust was the blood price to be paid in order for Israel to be born, but in the eyes of many the one event led directly to the other (Arnow, 1994). Some Zionists disagree, arguing that the development of the Jewish national movement was leading inexorably towards statehood regardless of the outcome of World War II. A consensus has yet to be reached (and might not be, given the passions involved on both sides of the argument), though in popular discourse the equation of the Holocaust with Israel has become increasingly entrenched (Friesler, 2008).

Regrettably, a further legacy of the Holocaust has seen the reappearance of antisemitism in the form of Holocaust denial, a movement that seeks to deny Nazi guilt by refusing to admit that it occurred, at the same time vilifying Jews worldwide in a crude attempt to discredit them while at the same time "denouncing" a massive Jewish "conspiracy" which aims to defraud the world (Lipstadt, 1993; Shermer and Grobman, 2000). Much of the deniers' strategy proceeds from a combination of falsification, deception, and half-truths, casting doubt on what they continually refer to as the "accepted version" of history (which plays further on the conspiracy notion). In this way, by casting doubt over accepted history, denial comes across as legitimate academic debate, enhancing the credibility of the deniers and devaluing the positions of authentic historians.

Denial of the Holocaust, tragically, might be seen as its final stage. It murders the dignity of the survivors, and destroys the remembrance of the crime. It strives to reshape history in order to rehabilitate the perpetrators and demonize the victims. And finally through the denial of the Holocaust (or any other genocides) a climate is created that can encourage fresh genocidal episodes elsewhere.

MEMORIALS AND MUSEUMS

Holocaust memorialization can be a highly complicated affair. How the Holocaust is publicly commemorated depends very largely on practical considerations, and in planning a memorial, logistical concerns abound. For example, who is commissioning the memorial? Is the intended location available, and, if so, is it appropriate? What is the budget within which those planning the memorial can operate? How is the memorial to be designed, and how are decisions to be made concerning its realization? Most importantly, in whose name does the planning committee speak— and to whom is the memorial directed (Young, 1993)?

Memorials are silent testaments to victimization and persecution, and while they express an important message—that of "we remember"—it could be argued that the only people for whom such remembrance really matters are the descendants of those slaughtered. For some Jews, the memorialization of the Holocaust is a matter for the interest of Jews alone, which is, of course, why an enormous amount of intellectual, financial, and emotional energy is directed towards Holocaust remembrance. Memorials are more numerous than museums and embrace a wide variety of types. These range through monuments, plaques, fountains, sculptures, statues, parks, and other public spaces designed to remember the Holocaust, some specific aspect of it, or people associated with it. Memorials can also include financial endowments, schools established after the war and dedicated to the memory of the Holocaust (especially among Jewish communities), organizations, scholarships, and the like.

Memorials to the Holocaust are many and range widely in style and size. Arguably the largest is the Memorial to the Murdered Jews of Europe, located in Berlin, Germany. Designed by architect Peter Eisenman and engineer Buro Happold, it consists of a 19,000-square-meter site covered with 2,711 concrete slabs arranged in a grid pattern on a sloping field. Building began on April 1, 2003, and was finished on December 15, 2004. It was dedicated on May 10, 2005—sixty years after the end of the war in Europe—and opened to the public two days later.

Among the large number of other memorials to the Holocaust (too numerous to mention here) are included the Judenplatz

Holocaust Memorial in Vienna, Austria; the Ghetto Heroes Monument in Warsaw, Poland; the Shoes on the Danube Promenade memorial in Budapest, Hungary; the Philadelphia Holocaust Memorial Plaza, in Philadelphia, Pennsylvania; and the Holocaust Memorial of the Greater Miami Jewish Federation, in Miami Beach, Florida (among many others). There are also memorials to the Holocaust in the Jewish sections of most city and suburban cemeteries.

Museums, like memorials, also have constraints imposed by finance, availability of locale, and questions of design and organization, but clearly the most fundamental difference between a memorial and a museum, so far as Holocaust commemoration is concerned, is that a museum display need not be a permanent statement in order to communicate its message, but can adapt to changing circumstances of time and purpose as desired. In this sense, a museum has a decided advantage in that it can act in a variety of roles: repository of material, educational tool, a focus for remembrance, and the location of an important cultural historic site. If purpose-built, it might well have a permanent exhibition and provision for additional exhibitions arranged according to changing themes or events. If it is not purpose-built but is, rather, devoted to a broader issue (such as with the Imperial War Museum in London), it might provide for the Holocaust or aspects of it in specific exhibitions. Either way, while political, planning, and financial considerations certainly come into play with the Holocaust-remembrance activities of museums, these are often overcome before there is a need for a project to be abandoned.

Museums to the Holocaust present specific problems. The Holocaust was a European experience of a very special kind, and such museums present Jews as a people marked by their experience of mass murder; quite simply, if Jews had not had that experience, there would not be Holocaust museums. Establishing museums which, focus simply on Jewish victimhood, therefore, can promote Jews as victims rather than giving them a status commensurate with other citizens; because of this, Holocaust museums can present awkward conceptual and display predicaments.

Clearly, the Holocaust deserves to be studied, written about and taught *because it happened*, but a sanctified shrine which eulogizes carnage and mass murder can serve to reduce visitors' grasp of the Holocaust to a benumbed apathy in which their perception of the events being witnessed takes on an air of unreality. Therefore, an enormous amount of care needs to be brought to the task of planning and arranging both the museum itself and the exhibitions it mounts. But there are those who argue that *something* must be done to commemorate lives lost, and to expose the barbarism that led to the destruction, and they, too, have a legitimate position. Extensive thought must be given to the question of just what it is that is being remembered; who is doing the remembering; and for what purpose the remembrance is taking place.

Yad Vashem, Israel's Holocaust Martyrs' and Heroes' Remembrance Authority, was established in 1953 by act of Israel's Knesset (parliament) to commemorate the victims of the Holocaust (Gutterman and Shalev, 2005). Located on the western slope of Mount Herzl on the Mount of Remembrance in Jerusalem, the site was chosen specifically because the area was not at that point crowded out with competing draws of historical significance. The site consists of a large complex containing the Holocaust History Museum, memorial sites such as the Children's Memorial and the Hall of Remembrance, the Museum of Holocaust Art, sculptures, outdoor commemorative sites such as the Valley of the Communities, a synagogue, a research institute with archives, a library, a publishing house, and the International School for Holocaust Studies.

The enormous United States Holocaust Memorial Museum, located on the National Mall in Washington D.C.—an idea initiated by President Jimmy Carter in 1978—was approved by Congress in 1980 (Linenthal, 2001). A grant of prime federal land on an outstanding site close to the Washington Monument led ultimately to the construction of a US$168 million state-of-the-art museum and educational complex dedicated to remembering and learning about the Holocaust, both as an historical event and as a bellwether for tolerance and democracy. Founded formally in 1993, the Museum is dedicated to presenting the history of the persecution and murder of 6 million Jews and millions of other victims as a result of Nazi tyranny from 1933 to 1945. The museum is comprised of a three-storey Permanent Exhibition which tells the story of the Holocaust through artifacts, photographs, films, and eyewitness testimony.

Holocaust museums exist in many countries around the world, not the least of which are in the places where the atrocities of the

Holocaust itself took place; hence, in former concentration camps (Auschwitz-Birkenau in Poland, and Dachau, Sachsenhausen, Buchenwald, Flossenbürg, Neuengamme, and Bergen-Belsen in Germany, among many others throughout Europe), as well as locations where key events took place (such as the Wannsee House, in Berlin and the Anne Frank House in Amsterdam), museums have been established to help the process of memorialization.

Every new attempt to establish a memorial or museum must begin anew the questioning process, and every case must be treated individually and on its merits. It is worth remembering, however, that the very first plan for a Holocaust museum was drawn up by the Nazis themselves. To stand in Prague, it was to be a collection of artifacts and images of Jews once they had been expunged from the face of the earth—a triumphant memorial to the Nazis' work of annihilation. It is not sufficient to say that simply exposing future generations to barbarism and evil is an antidote against it; after all, barbarians also learn from history.

LITERATURE AND FILM OF THE HOLOCAUST

The Holocaust is recalled in most expressions of popular culture, but as the distance in time from the event recedes, the two areas that will serve as the most likely repositories of memory will be literature and film.

The term "Holocaust literature" can be defined as the extensive body of written works, in many languages, which have responded to the Holocaust catastrophe. Such written works include diaries, creative writing, literary texts, compositions, informal literature, texts, reports, studies, poems, plays, leaflets, brochures, pamphlets, circulars, flyers, handouts, handbills, bulletins, fact sheets, publicity, propaganda, and notices. Most frequently, literary works on the Holocaust have been written in Hebrew, English, Yiddish, Polish, German, or French.

At the highest level, this literature provides readers with deep insights into the Holocaust through stories, poems, and plays that scrutinize events as they unfolded, and which suffering people experienced. Survivor testimonies play the most crucial role in forming our understanding of what life was like in the Nazi concentration camps. By virtue of their special status as first-hand narratives written by people who lived through the barbarities of the Nazi system, such testimonies are our primary link to the SS state as viewed from the victims' perspective. As such, all accounts, regardless of their artistic quality or historical accuracy, are nonetheless vitally important documents. These are the voices of the victims.

In the years immediately following World War II, writers began to confront the task of describing in fiction the seemingly indescribable and multifaceted world of the Holocaust. Even though some survivors immediately started to write of their experiences, many were unable even to speak about what they experienced. However, facing the inevitable reality of their own mortality, a number have since written testimonies detailing what they remember, in order to bear witness for future generations (Des Pres, 1976; Patterson, 1998).

Much Holocaust writing created by people other than survivors comes from Jewish writers attempting to generate their own understandings of the Holocaust phenomenon. Accordingly, many writers have fixed themselves on cases of unrecognized heroes of the Holocaust, both Jewish and non-Jewish, who resisted the Nazis.

Some literature has been created to teach children various ethical lessons stemming from the Holocaust, while other writing has set down the moral lessons that the world at large has to learn from this tragedy. Those who have attempted to address such issues have produced critical analyses, as well as fiction, drama, and poetry that honor the victims and survivors. Where the goal has been to prevent the recurrence of such a tragedy, other works have detailed the circumstances that permitted the rise of Nazism and its leaders during the period of the Third Reich.

Thousands of authors around the world have made the Holocaust the primary focus of their writing. Many are Jewish, such as Aharon Appelfeld, Elie Weisel, Tadeusz Borowski, Viktor Frankl, and Primo Levi. Others, whether Jewish or not, have utilized the Holocaust within their writing, while not necessarily classifying themselves as writers on the Holocaust. These include Yehuda Amichai, Cynthia Ozick, Jean-Paul Sartre, and William Styron. Academic scholars, such as Lawrence Langer, Sidra DeKoven Ezrahi, Sara Horowitz, Sue Vice, and James E. Young, have undertaken meticulous studies seeking to understand Holocaust literature and how it is to be best appreciated.

While any list of key texts on the Holocaust will always be contentious, at a minimum it might be argued that the following would likely be included in most collections if compiled in the early twenty-first century: Elie Wiesel, *Night*; Anne Frank, *The Diary of a Young Girl*; Art Spiegelman, *Maus*; Primo Levi, *If This Is a Man*; William Styron, *Sophie's Choice*; Bernhard Schlink, *The Reader*; Jonathan Safran Foer, *Everything Is Illuminated*; John Boyne, *The Boy in the Striped Pyjamas*; Sara Nomberg-Przytyk, *Auschwitz: True Tales from a Grotesque Land*; Anatoli Kuznetsov, *Babi Yar*; John Hersey, *The Wall*; and Markus Zusak, *The Book Thief*. Through Holocaust literature, readers can not only learn about the Nazi state and World War II, but also connect as human beings with those who lived and died during the Holocaust, as well as those who survived it.

As a subject for motion pictures, the Holocaust presents the broadest range of themes possible, covering nothing less than the entirety of the human experience *in extremis*—social, political, cultural, economic, military, administrative, religious, gender, age, race, and so on. The making, studying, and critiquing of film has become one of the largest and most popular contemporary ways of dealing with the Holocaust (Baron, 2005; Gonshak, 2015).

Filmographies covering the Holocaust are immense in size, and growing each year. For each film studied, the essential tools can remain the same, however. One must always be wary that the film-makers do not fall into the trap of maudlin sentimentality, as this can detract from the impact that a movie on the Holocaust can have on an audience—and, in particular, an uninformed or under-informed audience, such as those found among younger viewers today.

For the most part, however, it is simply not possible for film-makers to recreate with complete accuracy everything that happened in any historical situation, so liberties have to be taken—perhaps not with the truth, so much as with representations of the truth. While film-makers might have a commitment to telling the general outline of a story, in doing so they are often forced to select specific vignettes, themes, or exchanges in order to best express themselves (Rosenstone, 2006). The ambiguous caption "based on a true story" can lend credibility to the most tenuous of movie tie-ins, but film-makers seem generally content to employ the phrase if their movie has the remotest grounding in authenticity. More and more, indeed, even this has been expanded to include the term "inspired by real events."

Of course, there is a danger here; those who would detract or deny the veracity of the history being portrayed could well see that flaws in a movie generated by dramatic license can negate the entire account. But film-makers are, all too often, confined by the limits of their medium. An event relating to the Holocaust cannot be shown in all its shades and gradations in the space of 90 or 120 minutes. As a result, film-makers seek to interpret an incident or episode in accordance with the tools they have to hand. In this regard, the skills of the historian can meet those of the film-maker in order to produce works that enhance understanding of the Holocaust.

In approaching an issue such as the Holocaust, the study of film can be useful in providing a window to achieving a deeper understanding of why it is that such extraordinary violence took place. Nonetheless, a few questions—common to all students of film and its relationship to historical phenomena—can be asked in the hope that deeper insight can be achieved:

- How useful was the film in developing an understanding of the causes and nature of the Holocaust?
- Was more learned about the Holocaust from the film than from other sources of information?
- Did it appear to have any biases?
- Do any specific scenes best describe the overall topic of the movie?

The last three decades have seen a sharp increase in people's interest in the Holocaust, and motion pictures have been in the vanguard. Indeed, younger generations have probably learned more about the Holocaust through critical consumption of film than through any other medium, and are likely to glean much of their knowledge this way, both before and after their formal education.

The most fundamental of questions regarding filmic portrayals of historical issues can be addressed through a viewing of such movies: first, is the movie true to the historical reality (so far as it can be understood) upon which it is based? Second, is the movie useful in providing an understanding, for example, of what specific places or situations looked like? And third, how effective can graphic depictions of such situations be for a new generation of viewers seeing such images for the first time?

Movies stemming from Holocaust themes play an important role in helping to provide a sense of "place" and "period" for viewers. They are not documentaries, nor do they try to be. This is one of the major concerns some people have with regard to any movies that take historical episodes as their theme; namely, that because films employ actors speaking contrived dialogue, on movie sets that are recreations of what might have been, they have as little validity as if they were fiction. Yet an argument can be made that filmic portrayals of the Holocaust are often just as much an interpretation of historical realities as other forms of analysis—and in particular, of historical writing. They show, however, an image of reality, though not reality itself. Thus, while movies can be a start, they are not (and cannot be) the only medium for generating a full grasp of what that awful event signified—or of what it represents for the future of the world and the society in which viewers will be living once they leave the theater or turn off their television.

The Holocaust as a theme in motion pictures generated a number of important titles between the 1950s and the early 1990s. These included, but need not be restricted to, such movies as

- *The Diary of Anne Frank* (George Stevens, 1959),
- *Judgment at Nuremberg* (Stanley Kramer, 1961),
- *The Pawnbroker* (Sidney Lumet, 1964),
- *The Shop on Main Street* (Ján Kadár and Elmar Klos, 1965),
- *The Garden of the Finzi-Continis* (Vittorio De Sica, 1970),
- *The Last Metro* (François Truffaut, 1980),
- *Playing for Time* (Daniel Mann, 1980),
- *Sophie's Choice* (Alan J. Pakula, 1982),
- *Au Revoir Les Enfants* (Louis Malle, 1987),
- *The Nasty Girl* (Michael Verhoeven, 1990),
- *Europa, Europa* (Agnieszka Holland, 1991),
- *Korczak* (Andrzej Wajda, 1991).

Since then, the Holocaust has remained central, with interest in movies on the topic intensifying significantly after the appearance in 1993 of the multi-award-winning *Schindler's List*, directed by Steven Spielberg. Since that time, the genre has seen an escalation of major movies, many of which have won critical and popular acclaim; these include

- *Life Is Beautiful* (Roberto Benigni, 1997),
- *Sunshine* (István Szabó, 1999),
- *Conspiracy* (Frank Pierson 2001),
- *The Grey Zone* (Tim Blake Nelson, 2001),
- *Uprising* (Jon Avnet, 2001),
- *Amen* (Costa-Gavras, 2002),
- *The Pianist* (Roman Polanski, 2002),
- *Fateless* (Lajos Koltai, 2005),
- *Black Book* (Paul Verhoeven, 2006),
- *The Counterfeiters* (Stefan Ruzowitzky, 2007),
- *The Reader* (Stephen Daldry, 2008),
- *God on Trial* (Andy DeEmmony, 2008),
- *The Boy in the Striped Pajamas* (Mark Herman, 2008),
- *Defiance* (Edward Zwick, 2008),
- *Good* (Vicente Amorim, 2008),
- *Sarah's Key* (Gilles Paquet-Brenner, 2010),
- *La Rafle* (Rose Bosch, 2010),
- *In Darkness* (Agnieszka Holland, 2011),
- *Wunderkinder* (Markus Rosenmüller, 2011),
- *The Third Half* (Darko Mitrevski, 2012),
- *Ida* (Paweł Pawlikowski, 2013),
- *Son of Saul* (László Nemes, 2015).

GENERATIONS OF THE HOLOCAUST

As the mortality of the Holocaust generation approaches swiftly, the children of survivors, known collectively as the second generation, play an increasingly crucial role in keeping alive the memory of the Holocaust experience (Hass, 1996; Jilovsky, Silverstein, and Slucki, 2015). With many feeling as though they have been obligated to preserve their parents' memories, the responsibility is often quite crushing—no more so than because of what has come to be known in psychoanalytic literature as "transmitted trauma," anguish that is transferred from the survivors to their children (and, now, adult grandchildren) as a result of complex post-traumatic stress disorder (PTSD) processes. Most members of the second generation have been affected by their parents' experiences in one way or another, and to varying degrees.

Many view the Holocaust differently from their parents, often possessing a far more complex understanding of the Holocaust owing to a broader range of influences and approaches that have contributed to their knowledge of what happened during the war years. They are forced to assess the Holocaust in this different way while at the same time accepting that they must remain respectful of what they have been told as they were growing up, and not question the veracity of their parents' accounts of what happened.

There can be no doubt that many in the second generation carry conveyed emotional scars, frequently the result of their parents' untreated PTSD (Berger and Berger, 2001). Many Holocaust survivors suffered from life-long emotional and mental afflictions. As children, some in the second generation were embarrassed at their parents' passivity or victimization during the Holocaust; some also found unease as their parents displayed socially dysfunctional behavior out of alignment with the norms of wider society. For yet others, the question was not why their parents' experiences led them to be classed as socially aberrant, but rather, in view of all they had lived through, why they were so "normal." These issues have significantly affected some in the second generation, not only individually, but also in their relationships with their parents. Further, some in the second generation are also prone to emotional disturbances of their own bordering on a form of Holocaust-related PTSD, despite the fact that they did not experience the Holocaust themselves.

In recent times, consideration has also been made of the grandchildren of Holocaust survivors, the last generation of Jews who will have had any sort of direct link to the Holocaust.

While their experiences are for the most part less traumatic and more nuanced than those of their parents in the second generation, they are frequently just as committed to preserving Holocaust memory and communicating it to their own children and to the wider community with whom they interact. Often seeing themselves as the custodians of an important legacy, they are taking the first-person experiences of the Holocaust generation into the future so that after their grandparents have gone there will still be those who can say—deep into the twenty-first century—that they had personal experience with those who lived through the Holocaust.

DISCUSSION QUESTIONS

- Does Holocaust memory have a future? Why/Why not?
- "The Holocaust was so profound that only through ongoing educational efforts will its significance become apparent for future generations." Discuss this statement by reference to some of the key themes of Holocaust remembrance you have encountered.
- Are movies an effective means of conveying an understanding of the reality of the Holocaust?
- Should Holocaust literature be read, or studied? Explain why you think there might be a difference.
- How would you respond to a person who claimed that the Holocaust never happened?

GLOSSARY

Aktion A Nazi term for operations against Jews from villages or ghettos who were then assembled, deported to labor or death camps, and, in many cases, murdered

Allies The collective term for the countries fighting Nazi Germany, Italy, and Japan during World War II; these comprised primarily the United States, Britain and the Commonwealth, and the Soviet Union, with many other countries aligning with the aims of these major combatants

Anschluss German for "political union," used to describe the annexation of Austria by Germany on March 13, 1938

Antisemitism An umbrella term for a variety of negative beliefs or actions held or taken against Jews for the sole reason that they are Jewish

Aryan A term applied in Nazi ideology to people of Northern European racial background, in stark contradiction to other peoples (particularly Slavs, Latins, and especially Jews)

Concentration camp Camps established from 1933 onwards for the non-judicial imprisonment and forced labor of those identified by the Nazis as enemies of the Third Reich; these would ultimately include political opponents, Jehovah's Witnesses, Roma, homosexuals, so-called "asocials," and Jews

Crimes against Humanity A legal category within international law that identifies punishable offences for gross violations of human rights, atrocities, and mass murder of non-combatant civilians. Acts that can be considered as crimes against humanity include, but are not confined to, murder, extermination, enslavement, deportation, imprisonment, torture, rape, and persecutions on political, racial, and religious grounds

Death march Forced transfer and deportation of concentration camp inmates toward the end of World War II, undertaken to prevent their liberation by the Allies; these resulted in a vast number of deaths

Displaced Persons Survivors of the Holocaust or other World War II–related population dislocation at war's end, and who had no home to which they could immediately return

DP camps Special camps set up by the Allies to house, medically assist, and then enable Displaced Persons to find new homes, often outside of Europe

Einsatzgruppen SS mobile killing squads that followed the German military operations, largely in Poland and the Soviet Union after June 1941; supported by units of German police and local volunteers, they executed over a million Jews and others, mainly through shooting and the use of gas vans

Eugenics A pseudo-science focused on breeding "racially pure" human beings while at the same time "breeding out" so-called "defective" genes

Euthanasia In the Third Reich, the adoption of eugenic measures to improve the quality of the German "race" through the murder of those with incurable psychological problems, the permanently disabled, or those with physical and emotional disorders

Evian Conference An international conference convened by President Franklin D. Roosevelt in July 1938 to discuss the problem of Jewish refugees. Thirty-two countries met at Evian-les-Bains, France, but not much was accomplished (as was anticipated) owing to the reluctance of all those attending to accept Jewish refugees

Extermination camp A site to which Jews and others were deported for the purpose of their annihilation. The Nazis located six of these in occupied Poland: Auschwitz-Birkenau, Bełżec, Chełmno, Majdanek, Sobibór, and Treblinka

"Final Solution" The euphemistic cover name for the Nazi plan to exterminate the Jewish population of Europe (*Endlösung der Judenfrage*). Beginning in the late fall of 1941, Jews were rounded up in occupied German territories and sent to death camps to be murdered. To ensure compliance, they were told beforehand that they were going to be "resettled" in the East

Führer German word for "leader," the title by which Adolf Hitler was referred during the period of the Third Reich in Germany

Gas chamber A sealed room or other enclosed space in which a number of victims could be killed simultaneously by inhaling poison gas (such as carbon monoxide or by hydrocyanic acid (HCN), known by its commercial name of Zyklon B)

Genocide Any one of a number of acts committed with intent to destroy, in whole or in part, a national, ethnic, racial, or religious group, in accordance with the UN Convention on Genocide 1948

Gestapo Germany's secret state police force (*Geheime Staatspolizei*) and a branch of the SS, employed as a detective policing agency charged with creating a climate of fear and hunting down enemies of the state throughout occupied Europe

Ghetto A designated area where all Jews from a city and its surrounding areas were forced to reside. The ghetto would be surrounded by barbed wire or walls, and became a very clearly defined district, guarded from the outside. Established mostly in Eastern Europe, ghettos were usually sealed so that those imprisoned inside were prevented from leaving (or others from entering)

Holocaust One of the terms (along with *Shoah* and *Churban*) used to describe the destruction of approximately 6 million Jews by the Nazis and their collaborators in Europe and North Africa between the years 1933–1945. Among all those murdered by the Nazi regime during this period, only the Jews were marked for complete and utter annihilation

Jehovah's Witnesses A religious sect, originating in the United States, who refused to acknowledge the supremacy of the state over that of God. This brought them into conflict with the Nazi state which considered the Jehovah's Witnesses to be enemies; as a result, they were persecuted by the regime

Judenrat Jewish Council (plural, *Judenräte*), established by the Nazis in ghettos, especially in Eastern Europe. The role of the Council was to carry out German administrative directives, usually resulting in the deportation of the Jews prior to the ghetto's liquidation

Judenrein A term used to describe an area that has been cleansed or purified of all Jews by deportation and/or murder. Areas designated as having been "cleansed of Jews" were those where all Jews had been either murdered or deported

Kapo Concentration camp prisoners chosen to direct and discipline their fellow prisoners into complying with camp rules and regulations, allowing the camps to operate with fewer SS staff

Kristallnacht "Crystal Night" or "Night of Broken Glass" was a pogrom directed on November 9–10, 1938, throughout Germany and Austria by Nazis against Jews and conducted by SA forces and civilians. Synagogues were burned; Jewish homes, schools, and businesses were vandalized; 91 Jews were murdered. About 35,000 Jewish men were sent to labor or concentration camps

Labor camp Camp where Jews and other prisoners were forced to engage in hard labor in conditions of slavery

Lebensraum ("living space") A concept that flourished in Germany from the 1890s to the 1940s, which sought expand Germany's physical borders to accommodate a growing population, perceived as a matter of right for a "superior" people

Massacre The intentional, random, and often brutal killing of a significant number of relatively defenseless people, by a more powerful group or state force

Mein Kampf (*My Struggle*) An autobiographical book by Adolf Hitler written in 1923 while imprisoned after the Beer Hall Putsch, which outlined his vision for Germany. His racial ideology identified Germans as the master race entitled to *Lebensraum* in the East, in lands inhabited by so-called inferior Slavs

Nazi Member of the National Socialist German Workers' Party, which was founded after World War I and which Adolf Hitler led from 1921

Nuremberg Laws A series of antisemitic and racial laws in Nazi Germany. The first two of these laws were enacted by the Reichstag on September 15, 1935, at a special meeting convened during the annual Nuremberg Party Rally. These were the Law for the Protection of German Blood and German Honor, and the Reich Citizenship Law. These laws deprived German Jews of citizenship, removed Jews from German political, social, and economic life, and created definitions of Jewishness based on biological descent

Nuremberg Trials The prosecution by the Allies in 1945–1946 of the key Nazi leaders for crimes committed during World War II. Most were sentenced to imprisonment or death by hanging

Occupation A takeover of a country by a foreign power with the subsequent forceful control of that country's political, economic, and legal systems

Partisans Irregular soldiers or resistance fighters carrying out guerrilla warfare behind enemy lines

Persecution The systematic abuse of a person or group by others, usually based on difference in religion, race, or politics. The persecutor causes physical torment, harassment, isolation, imprisonment, fear, or pain, with the intention of causing severe suffering

Prejudice Pre-judgment of another person, community, or group, based on factors unrelated to merit or ability. Prejudicial conduct is based on accepting stereotypical misunderstandings, in conjunction with a tendency to single out those who differ from the majority

Pogrom A term usually associated with mob attacks against Jewish communities, it has also come to be applied more generally when violence takes place against any persecuted group. During much of the twentieth century, the term implied any attack on Jews regardless of the degree of official input, and irrespective of whether or not the attack was spontaneous or planned. The destruction wrought by pogroms varied from situation to situation, and could involve murder, rape, pillage, physical assault, and wanton or random destruction. Pogroms could also lead to genocidal massacres

Propaganda Biased information used to manipulate recipients and promote an agenda by generating an emotional rather than a rational response. Propaganda can be produced by governments, activist groups, companies, religious organizations, and the media through paintings, cartoons, posters, pamphlets, films, radio shows, television shows, and websites. The Nazis achieved the acceptance, amongst both opponents and admirers, of the most blatant falsehoods

Racism The prejudicial belief that biological characteristics such as skin pigmentation, facial features, bone structures, and hair quality are the primary determinant of human abilities, and that the human species is unequally divided along superior and inferior lines based on such attributes. Racism can lead to active forms of discrimination in the areas of politics, society, culture, economics, religion, and the military, and can be expressed through laws, socio-economic exclusion, discrimination, violence, and genocide

Refugee A person who has been forced to leave their nation, state, or place of living as a result of war or general unrest, cannot return home safely, and carries a well-founded fear of persecution should they attempt to do so

Reichstag The German parliament, which enacted Nazi laws from 1933–1945

Righteous among the Nations Non-Jews who, at the risk of their own lives, saved Jews from their Nazi persecutors

SA (*Sturmabteilung*) The Nazi Party's original paramilitary or storm-troopers, called "Brownshirts" from the color of their uniform. Organized in 1921, and led by Ernest Röhm, it supported Hitler's rise to power in the 1920s and 1930s by providing protection for Nazi rallies and assemblies, disrupting the meetings of opposing parties, fighting against the paramilitary units of the opposing parties, and boycotting Jewish businesses

Social Darwinism The late nineteenth century revision of Charles Darwin's "survival of the fittest" theory of evolution to create a belief that "superior" humans will overcome "sub-human" species

Sonderkommando The term given to work units in Nazi death camps, usually prisoners who were forced to work in the gas chambers, undressing rooms, and crematoria

SS (*Schutzstaffel*) Also called "Blackshirts" from the color of their uniform. From a small personal bodyguard unit for Hitler in 1925, the SS became a major paramilitary organization which was, from 1929 until the Nazi collapse in 1945, the primary agency of security, surveillance, and terror within Germany and German-occupied Europe. After Nazi Germany's defeat, the SS was judged by the International Military Tribunal at Nuremberg to be a criminal organization

Third Reich When Adolf Hitler became chancellor on January 30, 1933, the Nazi state was declared to be Germany's Third Reich (Empire), intended to last for a thousand years. The First Reich was the medieval Holy Roman Empire (800–1806). The Second Reich (1871–1918) was united Germany under the Hohenzollerns (1871–1918)

Totalitarianism A system of government in which no political or personal opposition is permitted, demanding total subservience on the part of individuals and institutions to the state. Totalitarian states are comprised of at least some of the following characteristics: a single-party state dominated by a single leader or a small clique; a weapons monopoly; a communications monopoly; a unifying ideology; an economic system that is either centrally directed, or in which the state plays a dominant role; a police presence that has permanently entrenched extraordinary powers of arrest; and the capacity to employ violence in order to uphold the authority of the state

Volk A Nazi concept relating to the emotional, ethnic, and national ties binding all Germans as a separate and distinct entity from others. The term implies a sense of racial purity and a uniquely distinctive Germanic culture. It provided an ideological foundation for Nazism and also for the Final Solution, underscoring the desirability of eliminating those who could never be part of the German people, and were by definition unassimilable

Wannsee Conference A meeting of senior government Nazi and SS leaders, held in the Berlin suburb of Wannsee on January 20, 1942. The meeting was called to ensure the cooperation of administrative leaders of various government departments in the implementation of the Final Solution and to resolve the means to be used for the killing process

War A state of organized, armed conflict between different states, or different groups within a state, that is usually open and declared. War is characterized by aggression and violence, is often prolonged, and is usually waged by military forces fighting against each other. Conflict taking place during war is typified by high mortality, economic and social disruption, and physical devastation in the areas where fighting takes place

War Crimes Acts committed during armed conflict that violate the international laws, treaties, customs, and practices governing military conflict between belligerent states or parties. War Crimes are a legal category within international law, identifying punishable offenses for serious violations (so-called "grave breaches") of the accepted international rules of war. War Crimes recognize individual criminal responsibility where such violations occur, enshrining the idea that individuals can be held accountable for their own actions during wartime, provided a moral choice was able to be made at the time of the offense

Weimar Republic The German democratic republic established in 1919, after World War I. Although economic conditions improved at a slow pace over the following years, Adolf Hitler was able to use rampant inflation and unemployment to bring about a demise of the Republic, which occurred when he became Chancellor in 1933

Yellow Star In Germany in 1937, Jewish prisoners in concentration camps were to wear a yellow triangle. By 1941 it was the standard emblem for all Jews over the age of six years throughout the Greater Reich. The yellow color was associated with cowardice. If caught outside the ghettoes for failing to wear it, Jews were subject to beatings, imprisonment, and sometimes worse. Inside the death camps, such visible badges of separation and identification were also in use. Though variations existed depending on the country under Nazi hegemony (sometimes the Star alone, sometimes with the word "*Jude*," "*Jood*," or *Juif*), it was the wearing itself that had the most obviously devastating effect

CHRONOLOGY

1919

January 5   The German Workers' Party (DAP) is founded by Anton Drexler and Karl Harrer

September 12   Adolf Hitler joins the DAP

1920

February 24   Nazi Party is established when the DAP is renamed; it becomes the National Socialist German Workers' Party (NSDAP); Hitler presents the 25-Point Program, the Nazi Party platform

1923

November 9   Hitler leads an attempt to overthrow the government of Bavaria; he fails

1924

February 24   Trial of Adolf Hitler for treason begins; he is found guilty, and sentenced to five years in prison

December 19   Hitler is released from Landsberg having served just eight months of his five-year sentence

1925

February 27 — Hitler declares the Nazi Party (NSDAP) to be re-established, with himself as leader (Führer)

1933

January 30 — Adolf Hitler is appointed Chancellor of Germany by President Paul von Hindenburg
February 27–28 — Reichstag fire; arrests of political opponents of the Nazis begin almost immediately
March 5 — Reichstag elections: Nazis gain 44 percent of vote in manipulated elections
March 20 — Dachau concentration camp is established
March 27 — The Enabling Act is passed
April 1 — Jewish businesses are boycotted across Germany
April 26 — Hermann Göring establishes the Gestapo
May 10 — Books written by Jews and "undesirables" are publicly burned
July 14 — The Law for the Prevention of Offspring with Hereditary Defects is passed, forcing many Germans with "undesirable genes" to be sterilized

1934

June 30 — *Sturmabteilung* (SA) leadership is purged during what becomes known as the Night of the Long Knives
August 2 — German president Paul von Hindenburg dies; Hitler declares the office of president abolished, and names himself Führer of Germany

1935

September 15 — The Nuremberg Laws are announced at the annual Party Rally

1936

July 1	Hitler Youth membership becomes compulsory for all "Aryan" boys
August 1	Summer Olympic Games begin in Berlin

1937

March 21	Papal encyclical *Mit Brennender Sorge* issued by Pope Pius XI
July 19	Buchenwald concentration camp is established

1938

March 12	The *Anschluss* (union) of Austria with Germany; all German antisemitic decrees are immediately applied to Austria
July 6–14	International conference on refugees held at Evian, France
August 1	Nazi Office of Jewish Emigration is established to speed up the pace of Jewish emigration from Germany
August 8	Mauthausen concentration camp is established in Austria
August 17	Nazis require Jewish women to add "Sarah" and men to add "Israel" to their names on all legal documents
August 19	Swiss government refuses entry to Austrian Jews seeking sanctuary
September 27	German Jews banned from practicing law
September 29–30	Munich Conference: Britain and France surrender the Sudetenland regions of Czechoslovakia to Germany by negotiation
October 5	Passports belonging to German Jews are marked with the letter "J" to indicate their identity
November 7	Ernst vom Rath, third secretary in the German Embassy in Paris, is shot and mortally wounded by Herschel Grynszpan; vom Rath dies on November 9, precipitating *Kristallnacht*

November 9–10	*Kristallnacht* pogrom occurs in Germany and Austria. Nazi figures give 91 Jews killed, and up to 10,000 are arrested; 267 synagogues are destroyed; figures are likely much higher

1939

March 15	Germany invades Czechoslovakia
May 15	The first prisoners arrive at Ravensbrück
June 17	The *S.S. St. Louis*, a ship carrying 936 Jewish passengers, returns to Europe after being denied entry into the United States and Cuba
August 23	The Nazi-Soviet Non-Aggression Pact is signed
September 1	Germany invades Poland; a curfew is imposed on German Jews
September 3	France and Britain declare war against Germany
September 17	Soviet Union invades Poland
September 21	Reinhard Heydrich orders *Einsatzgruppen* commanders to establish ghettos in German-occupied Poland
September 27	Warsaw surrenders; Jewish Councils are established in Poland
November 23	Yellow Stars are required to be worn by Polish Jews over the age of 10

1940

February 8	Łodz ghetto is established
April 1	Thousands of refugees are permitted into Shanghai, China
April 9	Denmark and southern Norway are invaded and occupied by Germany; Heinrich Himmler issues a directive to establish a concentration camp at Auschwitz
April 30	The Łodz ghetto is sealed off from the outside world
May 7	Nearly 165,000 inhabitants are sealed in the Łodz ghetto

May 10	France, the Netherlands, Belgium, and Luxembourg are invaded by Germany
May 20	Auschwitz concentration camp is established for Polish political prisoners
June 4	Neuengamme concentration camp opens
June 22	France surrenders to Germany; Marshal Philippe Pétain leads the pro-Nazi government established in Vichy
July 17	The first anti-Jewish measures are taken in Vichy France
September 7	German forces begin aerial bombings of Britain
October 3	Vichy France passes its own version of the Nuremberg Laws
October 16	Germans officially establish the Warsaw Ghetto
November 4	Jewish civil servants in the Netherlands are dismissed
November 16	The Warsaw Ghetto, containing nearly 500,000 Jews, is sealed

1941

January 21–26	Romanian Iron Guard annihilates hundreds of Jews
February 9	Dutch Nazis riot against Amsterdam Jews
March 1	Construction of Birkenau begins
April 21	Natzweiler-Struthof concentration camp opens in France
May 14	Over 4,000 Jews are rounded up in Paris at the Vel' d'Hiv
June 22	Germany violates its non-aggression pact with the Soviet Union and invades (Operation Barbarossa)
June 27	Białystok is occupied by the Nazis; Białystok ghetto is established
July 2	Ukrainian nationalists murder thousands in Lvov
July 17	*Einsatzgruppen* ordered to execute captured communists and Jews during Soviet campaign
July 20	Minsk ghetto is established
July 31	Adolf Eichmann appointed to prepare the "Final Solution"

September 1	The German euthanasia program is formally ended, following the deaths of some 100,000 people
September 6	The Vilna ghetto is established
September 19	Jews in Germany are ordered to wear yellow armbands bearing the Star of David
September 29	The *Einsatzgruppen* murders some 34,000 Jews at Babi Yar ravine, outside Kiev
October 7	Birkenau is established as the primary massmurder site of Auschwitz
October 22–24	Romanian and German forces massacre an estimated 50,000 Jews in Odessa
October 28	Approximately 9,000 Jews are killed outside of Kovno
November 8	Plans are made for the creation of a ghetto in Lvov
November 24	Terezín (Theresienstadt) ghetto/concentration camp is established
December 7	Japan attacks Pearl Harbor, drawing the United States directly into World War II
December 8	Chełmno extermination camp becomes fully operational; some 320,000 Jews will be murdered here
December 11	Germany and Italy declare war on the United States

1942

January 10	*Armée Juive* (Jewish Army) is created in France
January 20	Wannsee Conference takes place
January 16	Deportations from Łodz begin
February 23	Some 768 Jewish passengers, after being refused entry into Palestine, drown when the *S.S. Struma* sinks off of the Turkish coast
March 1	Extermination by gas begins at Sobibór
March 17	Killings begin at Bełżec extermination camp
June	First anti-Nazi resistance pamphlet is published by the White Rose group of Hans and Sophie Scholl

June 1	Jews in France, Holland, Belgium, Croatia, Slovakia, and Romania are ordered to wear Yellow Stars
June 1	Treblinka extermination camp begins operation
July 13	1,800 Jews are massacred in Jozefów, Poland, by German Reserve Police Battalion 101
July 14	Mass deportation of Dutch and Belgian Jews to Auschwitz begins
July 16	Over 4,000 children are taken from Paris and sent to Auschwitz; overall, some 12,887 Jews in Paris are sent through Drancy
July 22	Mass deportation of Jews from the Warsaw Ghetto to Treblinka begins
July 23	Adam Czerniakow commits suicide in Warsaw
July 28	The Jewish Combat Organization is formed in the Warsaw Ghetto
August 7	Dr. Janusz Korczak and 200 orphans under his care are gassed in Treblinka
August 17	Kurt Gerstein visits Bełzec death camp and witnesses the gassing of up to 3,000 Jews
August 29	The Reigner Telegram is sent
September 2–3	Revolt of the Łachwa ghetto, arguably the first ghetto revolt of the Holocaust
October 15	SS slaughters 25,000 Jews near Brest-Litovsk
October 25	Deportation of Norwegian Jews begins
October 28	First transport of Jews sent from Terezín (Theresienstadt) to Auschwitz
December 24	Armed operations by the Jewish Combat Organization against German troops in Kraków

1943

January 18–21	Renewed deportations of Jews from the Warsaw Ghetto begin following a visit from Himmler; Jewish resistance begins in the ghetto
February 22	Christoph Probst, Hans Scholl, and Sophie Scholl are executed after admitting to distributing White Rose pamphlets
February 26	The first Roma arrive at Auschwitz

March 13–14	Liquidation of the Kraków ghetto
March 23	Nazi deportation of Greek Jews begins
April 5	Approximately 4,000 Jews are massacred in the Ponary Forest, outside Vilna
April 19	New deportations from the Warsaw Ghetto; first day of Warsaw Ghetto Uprising; Britain and the United States begin the Bermuda Conference
May 1	Bermuda Conference ends
May 8	Nazi forces capture the Jewish Combat Organization's command bunker at Miła 18; Mordecai Anielewicz is among the dead found there
May 16	SS General Jürgen Stroop reports that the "Jewish quarter of Warsaw is no more"
May 19	Nazis declare Berlin to be *Judenfrei* ("cleansed of Jews")
June 2	3,000 Jews killed following resistance in Lvov; another 7,000 are sent to the concentration camp at Janowska
June 11	Himmler orders liquidation of all ghettos in occupied Poland
August 2	Treblinka uprising
August 15–16	Uprising of the Białystok ghetto
October 1–2	German police begin deportations of Danish Jews; Danes respond with a rescue effort that saves the lives of 90 percent of the Jewish population
October 14	Sobibór uprising
October 16	Major Nazi raid and *razzia* (round-up) against the Jews of Rome, who are sent to Auschwitz
October 21	Minsk ghetto liquidated

1944

January 22	U.S. president Franklin D. Roosevelt creates the War Refugee Board
March 19	Germany begins its occupation of Hungary; Adolf Eichmann is sent from Berlin to oversee the deportation of the Hungarian Jews

May 15	Beginning of the deportation of Jews from Hungary to Auschwitz; Jews from Ruthenia and Transylvania are deported
May 16	Germans offer to free 1 million Jews in exchange for 10,000 trucks
July 9	Raoul Wallenberg arrives in Hungary, where he distributes Swedish passports and sets up safe houses for Jews
July 11	Deportations from Hungary are halted by order of Regent Miklós Horthy
July 24	Majdanek extermination camp is liberated by the Russians
August 1–October 4	Warsaw Revolt
August 2	Germany destroys the so-called "Gypsy camp" at Auschwitz, gassing some 3,000 in the process
August 6	Łodz, the last Jewish ghetto in Poland, is liquidated with 60,000 Jews sent to Auschwitz
October 7	*Sonderkommando* revolt at Auschwitz; one of the gas chambers is destroyed, 15 SS guards and 400 members of the *Sonderkommando* are killed
November 8	Deportations resume in Budapest
November 19	The Vatican and four other neutral powers in Budapest issue a collective protest to the Hungarian government calling for the suspension of Jewish deportations
November 28	Himmler orders destruction of the gas chambers at Auschwitz
December 24–29	Hungarian Arrow Cross fascists attack Jews in Budapest

1945

January 5	Roza Robota, Estusia Wajcblum, Ala Gertner, and Regina Safirsztajn, accused of supplying gunpowder to the Auschwitz *Sonderkommando*, are executed

January 18	Evacuation of Auschwitz begins
January 19	Soviet Army liberates Łodz
January 28	Soviet forces liberate Auschwitz
April 9	Evacuation of Mauthausen begins
April 11	American forces liberate Buchenwald
April 15	British forces liberate Bergen-Belsen
April 27	Soviet forces liberate Sachsenhausen
April 29	American forces liberate Dachau; Soviet forces liberate Ravensbrück
April 30	Hitler commits suicide
May 1	Joseph Goebbels kills his wife and children before shooting himself as Berlin is surrounded by the Soviet Army
May 2	Soviet forces capture Berlin
May 3	Theresienstadt is surrendered to the International Committee of the Red Cross
May 5	American forces liberate Mauthausen
May 7	Germany surrenders to the Allies in Reims
May 9	Wilhelm Keitel signs surrender documents in Berlin
May 23	Heinrich Himmler commits suicide
September 1	Japan surrenders to the Allies after the United States detonates atomic bombs at Hiroshima and Nagasaki, ending World War II
October 18	International Military Tribunal of major war criminals begins at Nuremberg

1946

July 4	42 Jews are killed in a pogrom in Kielce, Poland
October 1	International Military Tribunal ends
October 15	Hermann Göring commits suicide in his cell at Nuremberg
October 16	Death sentences carried out at Nuremberg, as those condemned are hanged

BIBLIOGRAPHY

Abzug, Robert H. *Inside the Vicious Heart: Americans and the Liberation of Nazi Concentration Camps.* New York: Oxford University Press, 1985.

Adele, Wendy and Marie Sarti. *Women and Nazis: Perpetrators of Genocide and Other Crimes during Hitler's Regime, 1933–1945.* Palo Alto, CA: Academia Press, 2011.

Ainsztein, Reuben. *Jewish Resistance in Nazi-Occupied Eastern Europe: With a Historical Survey of the Jew as Fighter and Soldier in the Diaspora.* New York: Harper and Row, 1974.

Aly, Götz, Peter Chroust and Christian Pross. *Cleansing the Fatherland: Nazi Medicine and Racial Hygiene.* Baltimore, MD: Johns Hopkins University Press, 1994.

Arad, Yitzhak. *Belzec, Sobibor, Treblinka: The Operation Reinhard Death Camps.* Bloomington, IN: Indiana University Press, 1987.

Arendt, Hannah. *Eichmann in Jerusalem: A Report on the Banality of Evil.* New York: Viking, 1963.

Arnow, David. "The Holocaust and the Birth of Israel: Reassessing the Causal Relationship." *Journal of Israeli History*, 15:3 (1994), 257–281.

Bachrach, Susan and Steven Luckert. *State of Deception: The Power of Nazi Propaganda.* Washington, DC: United States Holocaust Memorial Museum, 2009.

Baron, Lawrence. *Projecting the Holocaust into the Present: The Changing Focus of Contemporary Holocaust Cinema.* Lanham, MD: Rowman and Littlefield, 2005.

Bartrop, Paul R. *Surviving the Camps: Unity in Adversity during the Holocaust.* Lanham, MD: University Press of America, 2000.

Bartrop, Paul R. (Ed.). *Encountering Genocide: Personal Accounts from Victims, Perpetrators, and Witnesses.* Santa Barbara, CA: ABC-CLIO, 2014.

Bartrop, Paul R. *Resisting the Holocaust: Upstanders, Partisans, and Survivors*. Santa Barbara, CA: ABC-CLIO, 2016.

Bartrop, Paul R. *The Evian Conference of 1938 and the Jewish Refugee Crisis*. Houndmills, UK: Palgrave Macmillan, 2018.

Bartrop, Paul R. and Eve E. Grimm. *Perpetrating the Holocaust: Leaders, Enablers, and Collaborators*. Santa Barbara, CA: ABC-CLIO, 2019.

Bauer, Yehuda. *Flight and Rescue: Brichah*. New York: Random House, 1970.

Bauer, Yehuda. *Jews for Sale? Nazi-Jewish Negotiations, 1933–1945*. New Haven, CT: Yale University Press, 1996.

Ben-Tov, Arieh. *Facing the Holocaust in Budapest: The International Committee of the Red Cross and the Jews in Hungary, 1943–1945*. Berlin: Springer-Verlag, 1988.

Berenbaum, Michael (Ed.). *A Mosaic of Victims: Non-Jews Persecuted and Murdered by the Nazis*. New York: New York University Press, 1990.

Berger, Alan and Naomi Berger (Eds.). *Second Generation Voices: Reflections by Children of Holocaust Survivors and Perpetrators*. Syracuse, NY: Syracuse University Press, 2001.

Berger, Zdena. *Tell Me Another Morning*. London: Michael Joseph, 1962.

Berkowitz, Michael. *The Crime of My Very Existence: Nazism and the Myth of Jewish Criminality*. Berkeley, CA: University of California Press, 2007.

Birenbaum, Halina. *Hope Is the Last to Die: A Personal Documentation of Nazi Terror*. New York: Twayne, 1971.

Blatman, Daniel. *The Death Marches: The Final Phase of Nazi Genocide*. Cambridge, MA: Harvard University Press, 2011.

Bloomstein, Rex (prod.). *Auschwitz and the Allies*. BBC Films, 1982.

Bracher, Karl Dietrich. *The German Dictatorship: The Origins, Structure, and Effects of National Socialism*. New York: Praeger, 1970.

Braham, Randolph L. *The Politics of Genocide: The Holocaust in Hungary*. Detroit, MI: Wayne State University Press, 2000.

Breitmann, Richard and Allan J. Lichtman. *FDR and the Jews*. Cambridge, MA: Harvard University Press, 2013.

Brenner, Reeve Robert. *The Faith and Doubt of Holocaust Survivors*. New York: Free Press, 1980.

Bridgman, Jon. *The End of the Holocaust: The Liberation of the Camps*. Portland, OR: Areopagitica Press, 1990.

Brothers, Eric. *Berlin Ghetto: Hernert Baum and the Anti-Fascist Resistance*. Stroud, UK: Spellmount, 2012.

Brown, Daniel Patrick. *The Beautiful Beast: The Life and Crimes of SS-Aufseherin Irma Grese*. Ventura, CA: Golden West Historical Publications, 1996.

Brown, Daniel Patrick. *The Camp Women: The Female Auxiliaries Who Assisted the SS in Running the Nazi Concentration Camp System*. Atglen, PA: Schiffer Publishing, 2002.
Browning, Christopher R. *Ordinary Men: Reserve Battalion 101 and the Final Solution in Poland*. New York: HarperCollins, 1992.
Browning, Christopher R. *The Origins of the Final Solution: The Evolution of Nazi Jewish Policy, September 1939–March 1942*. Lincoln, NE: University of Nebraska Press, 2004.
Burney, Christopher. *The Dungeon Democracy*. London: Heinemann, 1945.
Byers, Ann. *Saving Children from the Holocaust: The Kindertransport*. Buchanan, NY: Enslow, 2011.
Bytwerk, Randall L. *Julius Streicher: Nazi Editor of the Notorious Anti-Semitic Paper Der Stürmer*. New York: Cooper Square Press, 2001.
Ceffrey, Holly. *Doctor Josef Mengele: The Angel of Death*. New York: Rosen, 2001.
Cernyak-Spatz, Susan. *The Meeting: An Auschwitz Survivor Confronts an SS Physician*. Syracuse, NY: Syracuse University Press, 2000.
Cesarani, David and Suzanne Bargett (Eds.). *Belsen 1945: New Historical Perspectives*. London: Vallentine, Mitchell, 2006.
Cohen, Elie Aron. *The Abyss: A Confession*. New York: Norton, 1973.
Connelly, John. *From Enemy to Brother: The Revolution in Catholic Teaching on the Jews*. Cambridge, MA: Harvard University Press, 2012.
Conot, Robert E. *Justice at Nuremberg*. New York: HarperCollins, 1983.
Cornwell, John. *Hitler's Pope: The Secret History of Pius XII*. Boston, MA: Little, Brown. 1999.
Cutherbertson, Ken. *A Complex Fate: William L. Shirer and the American Century*. Montreal and Kingston: McGill-Queen's University Press, 2015.
Desbois, Fr. Patrick. *The Holocaust by Bullets: A Priest's Journey to Uncover the Truth behind the Murder of 1.5 Million Jews*. New York: Palgrave Macmillan, 2008.
Des Pres, Terrence. *The Survivor: An Anatomy of Life in the Death Camps*. New York: Oxford University Press, 1976.
d'Harcourt, Pierre. *The Real Enemy*. London: Longmans, Green, 1967.
Dillon, Christopher. *Dachau and the SS: A Schooling in Violence*. Oxford: Oxford University Press, 2015.
Dippel, John H. *Bound upon a Wheel of Fire: Why So Many German Jews Made the Tragic Decision to Remain in Nazi Germany*. New York: Basic Books, 1996.
Duffy, Peter. *Bielski Brothers: The True Story of Three Men Who Defied the Nazis, Saved 1,200 Jews and Built a Village in the Forest*. New York: HarperCollins, 2003.

Dumbach, Annette and Jud Newborn. *Sophie Scholl and the White Rose*. Oxford: One World, 2007.

Dvornik, Francis. *The Slavs in European History and Civilization*. New Brunswick, NJ: Rutgers University Press, 1986.

Dwork, Debórah and Robert Jan van Pelt. *Auschwitz: 1270 to the Present*. New York: Norton, 1996.

Dwork, Debórah and Robert Jan van Pelt. *Flight from the Reich: Refugee Jews, 1933–1946*. New York: Norton, 2009.

Edelheit, Abraham J. and Hershel Edelheit. *History of the Holocaust: A Handbook and Dictionary*. Boulder, CO: Westview Press, 1994.

Emanuel, Muriel and Vera Gissing. *Nicholas Winton and the Rescued Generations: Save One Life, Save the World*. London: Vallentine, Mitchell, 2011.

Favez, Jean-Claude. *The Red Cross and the Holocaust*. Cambridge: Cambridge University Press, 1999.

Feig, Konnilyn G. *Hitler's Death Camps: The Sanity of Madness*. New York: Holmes and Meier, 1979.

Feinberg, Ida Weisbaum and Maryann McLoughlin. *If the Dawn Is Late in Coming: Surviving Vilna and Vaivara*. Galloway, NJ: Richard Stockton College of New Jersey, 2008.

Fénelon, Fania. *Playing for Time*. New York: Atheneum, 1977.

Feng-Shan, Ho. *My Forty Years as a Diplomat*. Pittsburgh, PA: Dorrance Publishing, 2010.

Fest, Joachim C. *The Face of the Third Reich: Portraits of the Nazi Leadership*. London: Weidenfeld and Nicolson, 1970.

Flanagan, Ben and Donald Bloxham (Eds.). *Remembering Belsen: Eyewitnesses Record the Liberation*. London: Vallentine, Mitchell, 2005.

Fleming, Gerald. *Hitler and the Final Solution*. Berkeley, CA: University of California Press, 1984.

Friedlander, Henry. *The Origins of Nazi Genocide: From Euthanasia to the Final Solution*. Chapel Hill, NC: University of North Carolina Press, 1995.

Friedländer, Saul. *Kurt Gerstein: the Ambiguity of Good*. New York: Knopf, 1969.

Friedländer, Saul. *Nazi Germany and the Jews: The Years of Persecution, 1933–1939*. New York: HarperCollins, 1997.

Friedländer, Saul. *Nazi Germany and the Jews, 1939–1945: The Years of Extermination*. New York: HarperCollins, 2007.

Friesler, Evytar. "On the Myth of the Connection between the Holocaust and the Creation of Israel." *Israel Affairs*, 14:3 (2008), 446–466.

Fritzsche, Peter. *Life and Death in the Third Reich*. Cambridge, MA: Harvard University Press, 2008.

Garbe, Detlef. *Between Resistance and Martyrdom: Jehovah's Witnesses in the Third Reich*. Madison, WI: University of Wisconsin Press, 2008.

Garber, Zev. *Shoah. The Paradigmatic Genocide: Essays in Exegenisis and Eisagenisis*. Lanham, MD: University Press of America, 1994.

Gies, Miep. *Anne Frank Remembered*. New York: Simon and Schuster, 1987.

Gilbert, Martin. *Auschwitz and the Allies*. London: Martin Joseph/ Rainbird, 1981.

Gilbert, Martin. *The Righteous: The Unsung Heroes of the Holocaust*. London: Doubleday, 2002.

Gilbert, Martin. *Churchill and the Jews: A Lifelong Friendship*. New York: Henry Holt, 2007a.

Gilbert, Martin. *Kristallnacht: Prelude to Tragedy*. New York: Harper, 2007b.

Gilbert, Martin. *Beyond the Call of Duty: British Diplomats and Other Britons Who Helped Jews Escape from Nazi Tyranny*. London: British Foreign and Commonwealth Office, 2008.

Gjelsvik, Tore. *Norwegian Resistance, 1940–1945*. London: C. Hurst & Co, 1979.

Glantz, David M. *Operation Barbarossa: Nazi Germany's War in the East, 1941–1945*. Oxford: Oxford University Press, 2009.

Goldhagen, Daniel Jonah. *Hitler's Willing Executioners: Ordinary Germans and the Holocaust*. New York: Random House, 1996.

Gonshak, Henry. *Hollywood and the Holocaust*. Lanham, MD: Rowman and Littlefield, 2015.

Good, Michael. *The Search for Major Plagge: The Nazi Who Saved Jews*. New York: Fordham University Press, 2005.

Gordon, Sarah. *Hitler, Germans, and the "Jewish Question."* Princeton, NJ: Princeton University Press, 1984.

Gottesman, Shirley Berger and Maryann McLoughlin. *A Red Polka-Dotted Dress: A Memoir of Kanada II*. Galloway, NJ: Richard Stockton College of New Jersey, 2011.

Grau, Gunther and Claudia Schoppman. *The Hidden Holocaust: Gay and Lesbian Persecution in Nazi Germany, 1933–1945*. Chicago, IL: Fitzroy Dearborn, 1995.

Greenbaum, Masha. *The Jews of Lithuania: A History of a Remarkable Community, 1316–1945*. New York: Gefen, 1997.

Greenspan, Henry. *On Listening to Holocaust Survivors: Recounting and Life History*. Westport, CT: Praeger. 1998.

Gun, Nerin E. *The Day of the Americans*. New York: Fleet, 1966.

Gutman, Israel. *Resistance: The Warsaw Ghetto Uprising*. Boston, MA: Houghton Mifflin, 1994.

Gutterman, Bella and Avner Shalev. *To Bear Witness: Holocaust Remembrance at Yad Vashem*. Jerusalem: Yad Vashem, 2005.

Hale, Christopher. *Hitler's Foreign Executioners: Europe's Dirty Secret*. Stroud, UK: The History Press, 2011.

Hanser, Richard. *A Noble Treason: The Revolt of the Munich Students against Hitler*. San Francisco, CA: Ignatius Press, 2012.

Hardman, Leslie H. *The Survivors: The Story of the Belsen Remnant*. London: Vallentine, Mitchell, 1958.

Harvey, Elizabeth. *Women and the Nazi East: Agents and Witnesses of Germanization*. New Haven, CT: Yale University Press, 2003.

Hass, Aaron. *In the Shadow of the Holocaust: The Second Generation*. New York: Cambridge University Press, 1996.

Heimler, Eugene. *Concentration Camp*. London: Pyramid Books, 1961.

Helm, Sarah. *Ravensbrück: Life and Death in Hitler's Concentration Camp for Women*. New York: Nan E. Talese, 2014.

Herf, Jeffrey. *The Jewish Enemy: Nazi Propaganda during World War II and the Holocaust*. Cambridge, MA: Harvard University Press, 2006.

Hett, Benjamin Carter. *Burning the Reichstag: An Investigation into the Third Reich's Enduring Mystery*. Oxford: Oxford University Press, 2014.

Hoess, Rudolf. *Commandant of Auschwitz: The Autobiography of Rudolf Hoess*. Cleveland, OH: World Publishing Co., 1960.

Iancu, Michael. "Montpellier and Its Jews during World War II." *Studia Hebraica*, 8 (2008), 352–362.

Jasch, Hans-Christian, "Civil Service Lawyers and the Holocaust: The Case of Willian Stuckart." In Alan Steinweiss and Robert D. Rachlin (Eds.), *The Law in Nazi Germany: Ideology, Opportunism, and the Perversion of Justice*. New York: Berghahn, 2013, 37–61.

Jasch, Hans-Christian and Christopher Kreutzmüller (Eds.). *The Participants: The Men of the Wannsee Conference*. New York: Berghahn, 2017.

Jilovsky, Esther, Jordana Silverstein and David Slucki (Eds.). *In the Shadows of Memory: The Holocaust and the Third Generation*. London: Vallentine, Mitchell, 2015.

Joffroy, Pierre. *A Spy for God: The Ordeal of Kurt Gerstein*. New York: Harcourt Brace Jovanovich, 1971.

Kaplan, Marion A. *Between Dignity and Despair: Jewish Life in Nazi Germany*. New York: Oxford University Press, 1998.

Kedward, H.R. *In Search of the Maquis: Rural Resistance in Southern France, 1942–1944*. Oxford: Oxford University Press, 1993.

Kenrick, Donald and Grattan Puxon. *Gypsies under the Swastika*. Hatfield, UK: University of Hertfordshire Press, 2009.

Kershaw, Ian. *Hitler, 1889–1936: Hubris*. New York: Norton, 1999.

Kershaw, Ian. *Hitler, the Germans, and the Final Solution*. New Haven, CT: Yale University Press, 2008.

Koch, Hannsjoachim Wolfgang. *In the Name of the Volk: Political Justice in Hitler's Germany*. London: I.B.Tauris, 1997.

Langbein, Hermann. *Against All Hope: Resistance in the Nazi Concentration Camps, 1938–1945*. New York: Paragon House, 1994.

Laqueur, Walter (Ed.). *The Holocaust Encyclopedia*. New Haven, CT: Yale University Press, 2001.

Latané, Bibb and John M. Darley. *The Unresponsive Bystander: Why Doesn't He Help?* New York: Appleton-Century Crofts, 1970.

Latour, Anny. *The Jewish Resistance in France (1940–1944)*. New York: Holocaust Library, 1981.

Lawson, Tom. *Debates on the Holocaust*. Manchester: Manchester University Press, 2010.

Lazare, Lucien. *Rescue as Resistance: How Jewish Organizations Fought the Holocaust in France*. New York: Columbia University Press, 1996.

Lemkin, Raphael. *Axis Rule in Occupied Europe: Laws of Occupation, Analysis of Government, Proposals for Redress*. Washington, DC: Carnegie Endowment for International Peace, 1944.

Levi, Primo. *The Drowned and the Saved*. London: Sphere Books, 1989.

Lewinska, Pelagia. *Twenty Months at Auschwitz*. New York: Lyle Stuart, 1968.

Lewy, Guenter. *The Nazi Persecution of the Gypsies*. New York: Oxford University Press, 2001.

Lifton, Robert Jay. *The Nazi Doctors: Medical Killing and the Psychology of Genocide*. New York: Basic Books, 1986.

Linenthal, Edward T. *Preserving Memory: The Struggle to Create America's Holocaust Museum*. New York: Columbia University Press, 2001.

Lipstadt, Deborah. *Denying the Holocaust: The Growing Assault on Truth and Memory*. New York: Free Press, 1993.

Loeffel, Robert. *Family Punishment in Nazi Germany: Sippenhaft, Terror and Myth*. Houndmills, UK: Palgrave Macmillan, 2012.

Longerich, Peter. *Heinrich Himmler*. Oxford: Oxford University Press, 2012.

Lower, Wendy. *Hitler's Furies: German Women in the Nazi Killing Fields*. Boston, MA: Houghton Mifflin Harcourt, 2013.

Maccoby, Hyam. *Antisemitism and Modernity: Innovation and Continuity*. Abingdon, UK: Routledge, 2006.

Maijer, Diemut. *"Non Germans" under the Third Reich: The Nazi Judicial and Administrative System in Germany and Occupied Eastern Europe, with Special Regard to Occupied Poland, 1933–1945*. Baltimore, MD: Johns Hopkins University Press, 2003.

Mailänder, Elissa. *Female SS Guards and Workday Violence: The Majdanek Concentration Camp, 1942–1944*. East Lansing, MI: Michigan State University Press, 2015.

Margolis, Heda. *I Do Not Want to Remember: Auschwitz 1941–Prague 1968*. London: Weidnefeld and Nicolson, 1973.

McKale, Donald M. *The Nazi Party Courts: Hitler's Management of Conflict in His Movement, 1921–1945*. Lawrence, KS: University Press of Kansas, 1974.

Miller, Richard M. *Nazi Justiz: Law of the Holocaust*. Westport, CT: Praeger, 1995.

Moczarski, Kazimierz. *Conversations with an Executioner*. Englewood Cliffs, NJ: Prentice-Hall, 1981.

Müller, Filip. *Eyewitness Auschwitz: Three Years in the Gas Chambers*. Chicago, IL: Ivan R. Dee, 1979.

Müller, Ingo. *Hitler's Justice: The Courts of the Third Reich*. Cambridge, MA: Harvard University Press, 1991.

Muller, Melissa. *Anne Frank: The Biography*. New York: Metropolitan Books, 1998.

Nansen, Odd. *Day after Day*. London: Putnam, 1949.

Novick, Peter. *The Holocaust in American Life*. Boston, MA: Houghton Mifflin, 1999.

Nyholm, Ove (prod.). *Anatomy of Evil (Ondskabens Anatomi)*. Angel Films, 2005.

Orlov, Dietrich. *The Nazi Party 1919–1945: A Complete History*. New York: Enigma Books, 2008.

Paldiel, Mordecai. *The Path of the Righteous: Gentile Rescuers of Jews during the Holocaust*. Hoboken, NJ: KTAV, 1993.

Paldiel, Mordecai. *Saving the Jews: Amazing Stories of Men and Women Who Defied the "Final Solution."* Rockville, MD: Schreiber Publishing, 2000.

Paldiel, Mordecai. *Diplomat Heroes of the Holocaust*. New York: Yeshiva University/KTAV, 2007a.

Paldiel, Mordecai. *The Righteous Among the Nations: Rescuers of Jews during the Holocaust*. New York: Harper and Row, 2007b.

Paldiel, Mordecai. *Saving One's Own: Jewish Rescuers during the Holocaust*. Philadelphia, PA: Jewish Publication Society, 2017.

Pasher, Yoram. *Holocaust versus Wehrmacht: How Hitler's "Final Solution" Undermined the German War Effort*. Lawrence, KS: University Press of Kansas, 2014.

Patterson, David. *Sun Turned to Darkness: Memory and Recovery in the Holocaust Memoir*. Syracuse, NY: Syracuse University Press, 1998.

Pawlowicz, Sala. *I Will Survive*. London: Muller, 1964.

Penkower, Monty Noam. *The Jews Were Expendable: Free World Diplomacy and the Holocaust*. Champaign, IL: University of Illinois Press, 1983.

Perl, Gisella. *I Was a Doctor in Auschwitz*. New York: International Universities Press, 1948.

Persico, Joseph E. *Nuremberg: Infamy on Trial*. New York: Viking Penguin, 1994.

Pilecki, Witold. *The Auschwitz Volunteer: Beyond Bravery*. Los Angeles, CA: Aquila Polinica, 2012.

Pilyar, Yuri. *It All Really Happened*. Moscow: Foreign Languages Publishing House, 1960.

Pinson, Koppel S. "Simon Dubnow: Historian and Political Philosopher." In Koppel S. Pinson (Ed.), *Simon Dubnow, Nationalism and History: Essays on Old New Judaism*. New York: Atheneum, 1970, pp. 3–65.

Plant, Richard. *The Pink Triangle: The Nazi War Against Homosexuals*. New York: Henry Holt, 1986.

Posner, Gerald L. and John Ware. *Mengele: The Complete Story*. New York: Cooper Square Press, 2000.

Proctor, Robert. *Racial Hygiene: Medicine under the Nazis*. Cambridge, MA: Harvard University Press. 1988.

Rabinowitz, Dorothy. *New Lives: Survivors of the Holocaust Living in America*. New York: Knopf, 1976.

Rashke, Richard. *Escape from Sobibor*. London: Michael Joseph, 2013.

Reeves, T. Zane. *Shoes along the Danube: Based on a True Story*. Durham, CT: Strategic Book Group, 2011.

Rhodes, Richard. *Masters of Death: The SS-Einsatzgruppen and the Invention of the Holocaust*. New York: Knopf, 2002.

Riegner, Gerhart M. *Never Despair: Sixty Years in the Service of the Jewish People and the Cause of Human Rights*. Chicago, IL: Ivan R. Dee, 2006.

Rings, Werner. *Life with the Enemy: Collaboration and Resistance in Hitler's Europe, 1939–1945*. Garden City, NY: Doubleday, 1982.

Robinson, Ritchie. *The "Jewish Question" in German Literature, 1749–1939: Emancipation and Its Discontents*. Oxford: Oxford University Press, 2001.

Roseman, Mark. *The Villa, the Lake, the Meeting. Wannsee and the Final Solution*. London: Allen Lane, 2002.

Rosenbaum, Alan S. (Ed.). *Is the Holocaust Unique? Perspectives on Comparative Genocide*. (3rd edition). Boulder, CO: Western Press, 2018.

Rosenstone, Robert A. *History on Film/Film on History*. Harlow, UK: Pearson Longman, 2006.

Roudinesco, Elizabeth. *Revisiting the Jewish Question*. Cambridge: Polity Press, 2014.

Rousset, David. *A World Apart*. London: Secker and Warburg, 1951.

Rubenstein, Richard L. and John K. Roth (Eds.). *Approaches to Auschwitz: The Holocaust and Its Legacy*. Louisville, KY: Westminster John Knox Press, 2003.

Salvesen, Sylvia. *Forgive, but Do Not Forget*. London: Hutchinson, 1958.

Samuels, Diane. *Kindertransport*. London: Nick Hern Books, 2010.

Schleunes, Karl A. *The Twisted Road to Auschwitz: Nazi Policy toward German Jews, 1933–1939*. Urbana, IL: University of Illinois Press, 1970.

Semprun, Jorge. *The Long Voyage*. London: Weidenfeld and Nicolson, 1963.

Shephard, Ben. *After Daybreak: The Liberation of Belsen, 1945*. London: Pimlico, 2006.

Shermer, Michael and Alex Grobman. *Denying History: Who Says the Holocaust Never Happened and Why Do They Say It?* Berkeley, CA: University of California Press, 2000.

Silver, Eric. *The Book of the Just: The Unsung Heroes Who Rescued Jews from Hitler*. New York: Grove Press, 1992.

Sofsky, Wolfgang. *The Order of Terror: The Concentration Camp*. Princeton, NJ: Princeton University Press, 1997.

Spiegel, Fred. *Once the Acacias Bloomed: Memories of a Childhood Lost*. Galloway, NJ: Richard Stockton College of New Jersey, 2004.

Stahel, David. *Operation Barbarossa and Germany's Defeat in the East*. Cambridge: Cambridge University Press, 2009.

Stangneth, Bettina. *Eichmann before Jerusalem: The Unexamined Life of a Mass Murderer*. New York: Knopf, 2014.

Stegelmann, Katherine. *Staying Human: The Story of a Quiet World War II Hero*. New York: Skyhorse Publishing, 2014.

Stevens, Lewis M. "The Life and Character of Earl G. Harrison." *University of Pennsylvania Law Review*, 104:5 (March 1956), 591–602.

Stolleis, Michael. *The Law under the Swastika: Studies on Legal History in Nazi Germany*. Chicago, IL: University of Chicago Press, 1998.

Stone, Dan. *Histories of the Holocaust*. Manchester: Manchester University Press, 2010.

Stone, Dan. *The Liberation of the Camps: The End of the Holocaust and Its Aftermath*. New Haven, CT: Yale University Press, 2015.

Stroop, Jürgen. *The Stroop Report: The Jewish Quarter of Warsaw Is No More!* New York: Pantheon Books, 1979.

Strzelecki, Andrzej. *The Evacuation, Liquidation, and Liberation of Auschwitz*. Oświęcimia, Poland: Auschwitz-Birkenau State Museum, 2008.

Szmaglewska, Seweryna. *Smoke over Birkenau*. New York: Henry Holt, 1947.

Tec, Nechama. *When Light Pierced the Darkness: Christian Rescuers of Jews in Nazi-Occupied Poland*. New York: Oxford University Press, 1986.

Tec, Nechama. *Defiance: The Bielski Partisans*. New York: Oxford University Press, 1993.

Tec, Nechama. *Resistance: Jews and Christians who Defied the Nazi Terror*. Oxford: Oxford University Press, 2013.

Thalmann, Rita and Emmanuel Feinermann, *Crystal Night: 9–10 November 1938*. New York: Coward, McCann and Geoghegan, 1974.

Tillion, Germaine. *Ravensbrück*. Garden City, NY: Anchor Books/Doubleday,1975.

Todorov, Tzvetan. *Facing the Extreme: Moral Life in the Concentration Camps*. New York: Henry Holt, 1996.

Trunk, Isaiah. *Jewish Responses to Nazi Persecution: Collective and Individual Behavior in Extremis*. New York: Stein and Day, 1979.

Unsdorfer, S. B. *The Yellow Star*. New York: Thomas Yoseloff, 1961.

Venezia, Shlomo. *Inside the Gas Chambers: Eight Months in the Sonderkommando in at Auschwitz*. Cambridge: Polity Press, 2011.

Vromen, Suzanne. *Hidden Children of the Holocaust: Belgian Nuns and Their Daring Rescue of Young Jews from the Nazis*. Oxford: Oxford University Press, 2008.

Wachsmann, Nikolaus. *KL: A History of the Nazi Concentration Camps*. New York: Farrar, Straus and Giroux, 2015.

Weale, Adrian. *Army of Evil: A History of the SS*. New York: NAL Caliber, 2010.

Weindling, Paul. *Victims and Survivors of Nazi Human Experiments: Suffering and Science in the Holocaust*. London: Bloomsbury, 2015.

Weisberg, Alex. *Desperate Mission: Joel Brand's Story*. Vancouver: Criterion Books, 1958.

Weiss, Reska. *Journey Through Hell: A Woman's Account of Her Experiences at the Hands of the Nazis*. London: Vallentine, Mitchell, 1961.

Welch, David. *Propaganda and the German Cinema, 1933–1935*. London: I. B. Tauris, 1983.

Welch, David. *The Third Reich: Politics and Propaganda*. London: Routledge, 1993.

Wick, Steve. *The Long Night: William L. Shirer and the Rise and Fall of the Third Reich*. New York: Palgrave Macmillan, 2011.

Wiesel, Elie. "Art and Culture after the Holocaust." *Cross Currents*, 26:3 (Fall 1976), 258–269.

Wistrich, Robert S. *A Lethal Obsession: Anti-Semitism from Antiquity to the Global Jihad*. New York: Random House, 2010.

Wrobel, Eta. *My Life My Way: The Extraordinary Memoir of a Jewish Partisan in WWII Poland*. Paradise Valley, PA: The Wordsmithy, 2006.

Wünschmann, Kim. *Before Auschwitz: Prisoners in the Prewar Concentration Camps*. Cambridge, MA: Harvard University Press, 2015.

Wyman, David S. *The Abandonment of the Jews. America and the Holocaust, 1941–1945*. New York: Norton, 1984.

Wyman, Mark. *DPs: Europe's Displaced Persons, 1945–51*. Ithaca, NY: Cornell University Press, 1998.

Yahil, Leni. *The Holocaust: The Fate of European Jewry, 1932–1945*. New York: Oxford University Press, 1990.

Young, James E. *The Texture of Memory: Holocaust Memorials and Meaning*. New Haven, CT: Yale University Press, 1993.

Zuccotti, Susan. *Under His Very Windows: The Vatican and the Holocaust in Italy*. New Haven, CT: Yale University Press, 2000.

Zuckerman, Yitzhak. *A Surplus of Memory: Chronicle of the Warsaw Ghetto Uprising*. Berkeley, CA: University of California Press, 1993.

Zywulska, Krystyna. *I Came Back*. London: Dennis Dobson, 1951.

INDEX

Abadi, Moussa 67
Aliens Law 52
Anielewicz, Mordecai 112
Antisemitic German Social Party 51
antisemitism 16–17, 26, 27–29, 51–52
Antyfaszystowska Organizacja Bojowa (Anti-Fascist Military Organisation; AOB) 97
Arendt, Hannah 35
Armée Juive (Jewish Army; AJ) 107–108
Arrow Cross (Nyilas) Party 23, 74–75
Atlas, Icheskel 98
Auschwitz/Auschwitz-Birkenau: in camp system 6, 12; evacuation of 132; female guards at 37–39; Hoess at 31, 32–34; Hungarian campaign and 14; liberation of 119, 138; prisoner rebellions at 97, 101, 113–114; Roma and 61; Westerbork and 57
Axis Rule in Occupied Europe (Lemkin) 129

Bachner, Wilhelm 67
Balfour Declaration 147
Bauer, Bruno 50
Baum, Bruno 114
Baum, Herbert and Marianne 97

Becker-Freyseng, Hermann 40
Bełżec 5, 6, 12, 14, 91, 115, 119
Bérenger, Henry 78
Bergen-Belsen 15, 56, 59, 119, 121–123
Berger, Ernst 114
Bermuda Conference 93–94
Bernburg 55
Bielski brothers 98, 103–106
Binz, Dorothea 37, 38
Birenbaum, Halina 132–133, 134, 140
Birkenau 12, 32–33, 37, 114, 135, 137–138; *see also* Auschwitz/Auschwitz-Birkenau
Black Death 16
"Blood for Goods" scheme 94
Bogaard, Aagje 71
Bogaard, Antheunius 71–72
Bogaard, Johannes 70–72
Bogaard, Johannes, Sr. ("Grandpa") 71–72
Bogaard, Klassje 72
Bogaard, Metje 71–72
Bogaard, Pieter 72
Bogaard, Willem 71–72
Bolshevik ideology 18
Börgermoor 9
Bormann, Juana 37
Bormann, Martin 31

Bouhler, Philipp 55
Bradley, Omar 119
Brandenburg 55
Brandt, Karl 55
Bricha (escape) 125
Bridgman, Jon 118
British Association for Holocaust Studies 146
British diplomats and *Kristallnacht* 80–82
Browning, Christopher 34–35
Buchenwald 15, 119, 131, 142
Burney, Christopher 142
bystanders 86–88

Calmeyer, Hans 90
carbon monoxide 14
Carter, Jimmy 150
Carvell, John 81
Central Office for Jewish Emigration 84–86
Chamberlain, Houston Stewart 51
Chamberlain, Neville 83
Charter of the Nuremberg Trials 21
Chełmno 6, 12, 14, 61, 115
children: experience of 12–13; *Kindertransport* for 82–84; number of, as victims 8
Churban (catastrophe) 8
Churchill, Winston 129
civil rights movement 21
Cohen, Elie Aron 136
Cohn, Marianne 67, 108–109
collaborators: corporate 30, 34; desk killers 35–36; legal professionals 41–45; medical professionals 39–41; outside Germany 45–46; Reserve Police Battalion 101 34–35; unwilling Jews as 47–48; women 36–39
"Common Plan, The" 126, 127–128
concentration camps 5–6, 9, 113–115, 118–119; *see also* death camps

Convention on the Prevention and Punishment of the Crime of Genocide 21, 130
cooperation 30, 34
corporations, German 30, 34
crematoria 13, 33, 114, 118
Crimes against Humanity 127, 128
Crimes against Peace 126, 128
Cyrankiewicz, Jozef 113–114

Dachau 9, 15, 31, 119, 131, 136
Daluege, Kurt 26
de Lagarde, Paul 51
death camps 5–6, 12–14, 24–25, 26, 118–119
death marches 14–15, 117–118, 120, 131–134
Decree for the Protection of the People and the State 9
"defective" people 3
dehumanization 27
Depression 18
Der Stürmer 27
desk killers 35–36
Dillon, Christopher 36
Displaced Persons' (DP) camps 123–126
Dowden, Arthur 81
Drexler, Anton 52
Drossel, Heinz 75–76
Dubnow, Simon 1–2
Dubois, Stanislaw 113
Düring, Karl Eugen 51

Eckstein, Dr. 142, 143
Eichmann, Adolf 32, 35–36, 83, 84–85, 94
Eicke, Theodor 31
Einsatzgruppen (Special Action Groups) 11–12, 18, 24, 26, 29
Eisenhower, Dwight D. 119, 124–125
Eisenman, Peter 148
emigration, facilitation of 84–86
Enabling Act 42

Enlightenment 16
Errázuriz, María 67
Esterwegen 9
eugenics 17, 20, 54
Euthanasia (*Aktion T4*) Program 18, 39, 55–56
evacuations, forced *see* death marches
Evian Conference 76–80
Ewige Jude, Die (The Eternal Jew) 28
experimentation on human subjects 39–41
extermination camps *see* death camps

false documents and forgery 108–109
Farben, I.G. 33
Fareynikte Partizaner Organizatsie (United Partisan Organization; FPO) 97
Feinberg, Ida Weisbaum 119–121
Feinberg, Sender 119, 121
female guards 36–39
Fénelon, Fania 3–4
films: on Holocaust 153–156; as propaganda 28
Flossenbürg 119
Föhrenwald 126
Fontheim, Ernst 76
Frank, Anne 66, 70
Frank, Hans 25
freedom 137–138
Freikorps 31
Freisler, Roland 44–45
French Resistance 111
Fritzsch, Theodor 51
Führerbefehl (Führer Order) 18
Fulham, Frank 81
functionalists 15–16

gas chambers 13, 14, 32–33, 39, 118
gas vans 11–12
Gebelev, Mihail 97
Gebhardt, Karl 41
Gemlich, Adolf 51
Gemmeker, Albert 59

genocide: international legislation on 4; origin of term 129–130; policy of 50; uniqueness of 4–5
Gerstein, Kurt 91
Gerstein Report 91
Gertner, Ala 114
Ghetto Heroes Monument 149
ghettos 11, 97, 102, 111–112
Gies, Miep 66, 70
Gildenman, Moshe 98
Giniewski, Otto ("Toto") 109
Giniewski, Paul 109
Glücks, Richard 33
Goebbels, Josef 24, 25, 27–28
Goldhagen, Daniel 35
Göring, Hermann 10–11, 24
Gottesman, Shirley Berger 12–13
Grafeneck 55
Grese, Irma 37–38
grey zone 47–48
Grini prison 141
Grünhut, Aron 67
Gryn, Hugo 47–48
Grynszpan, Herschel 10

Hadamar 55
Halifax, Viscount 80
Happold, Buro 148
Hardman, Leslie 122–123
Harrison, Earl G. 124
Hartheim 55
Harvey, Elizabeth 36
Hashomer Hatzair 110
Hass family 76
Hebrew Immigration Aid Society (HIAS) 83
Heimler, Eugene 142, 143
Henderson, Nevile 80
Hensel, Hedwig 31
Heydrich, Reinhard 5, 24, 26, 35
Himmler, Heinrich: establishment of camps and 9; Hoess and 32; prisoner rebellions and 115; Roma and 61; SS and 5, 24, 26; suicide of

25; Warsaw Ghetto Uprising and 112; women as perpetrators and 36
Hindenburg, Paul von 8–9
Hippler, Fritz 28
Hirschfeld, Marianne 75, 76
Hitler, Adolf: causes of Holocaust and 15–16, 18–19; dehumanization of Jews by 27; Evian Conference and 80; Hoess and 31; as instigator of Holocaust 26; on Jewish Question 51–52; judicial system and 42, 44; perpetrators of Holocaust and 3, 24; propaganda and 27–28; Reichstag fire and 8–9; 25 Points and 52–54; Versailles and 17
Hitler's Willing Executioners (Goldhagen) 35
Hlinka Guard 23
Ho Feng-Shan 66–67
Hoare, Samuel 81
Hoess, Rudolf Franz 31–34
Holocaust: causes and consequences of 8–21; ending 117–130; introduction to 1–7; perpetrators of 23–48, 89–92; remembering 145–158; rescue from the Third Reich and 66–95; resistance during 96–116; survivors' reflections on 131–143; victims of 19, 49–65
Holocaust denial 147
Holocaust Memorial of the Greater Miami Jewish Federation 149
Holocaust Studies: A Journal of Culture and History 146
Holuj, Tadeusz 114
homosexuals 62–63
Horthy, Miklós 74
human condition 141–143
Hungarian campaign 14
hydrocyanic acid gas 14
hydrogen cyanide 14

industrialization 18
intentionalists 15

International Association of Genocide Scholars (IAGS) 145–146
International Committee of the Red Cross (ICRC) 15, 94–95
International Criminal Court 21
International Military Tribunal (IMT) 21, 25, 126–128
International Network of Genocide Scholars 146
international response 76–80, 92–95
Israel 20, 125, 147

Jabotinsky, Vladimir 107
Jecklen, Friedrich 112
Jefroykin, Jules ("Dika") 108
Jehovah's Witnesses 63–64
"Jew Bill" (Jewish Nationalization Act; England; 1753) 50
Jewish Councils (*Judenräte*) 47, 58
Jewish Fighting Organization (Żydowska Organizacja Bojowa; ŻOB) 111–112
"Jewish Question" (*Judenfrage*) 50–52, 54
Jewish Question, The (Bauer) 50
Jonas, Regina 67
Judenplatz Holocaust Memorial 148–149
judges 42
judicial system 41–45

K., Elizabeth 140
Kampfgruppe Auschwitz (Auschwitz Combat Section) 113–114
Kanada 12–13
Kemna 9
killing culture 29
Kindertransport 82–84
Knut, Ariane 106–107
Knut, Dovid 106–107
Kommissarbefehl (Commissar Order) 18
Kovner, Abba 97
Kramer, Joseph 121–122
Kreyssig, Lothar 45

Kristallnacht (Night of Broken Glass) 10–11, 56, 80–82

Łachwa 97
Lalleri 61
Langbein, Hermann 113, 114
Law against Dangerous and Habitual Criminals 61
Law for the Prevention of Offspring with Hereditary Diseases/Defects 55, 61
League of Nations High Commission 78, 79
legal professionals 41–45
Lemkin, Raphael 129–130
Levi, Primo 47
Lévitte, Simon 108–109
liberation of camps 118–119
Lichtenburg 9, 36–37, 38
"life unworthy of life" (*Lebensunwertes Leben*) 3, 39, 55–56
Lill, Karl 114
literature and film 151–156
London Charter 126
Lopatyn, Dov 97
Lösener, Bernhard 44
Lower, Wendy 36
Lublin, (Aron) Lucien 106, 107
luck 136–137
Lutz, Carl 70

Main Forte, La (The Strong Hand) 106
Majdanek 6, 12, 14, 61, 102, 118
Mandl, Maria 38–39
Margolius, Heda 133
Marr, Wilhelm 51
Marx, Karl 50–51
Mauthausen 15
Mayr, Karl 51
medical professionals 39–41
Medicus, Franz Albrecht 44
Mein Kampf (Hitler) 28, 52
Memorial to the Murdered Jews of Europe 148

memorials and museums 148–151
Mengele, Josef 40
military experiments 40
Ministry of Public Enlightenment and Propaganda 27–28
misinformation 28
mobile killing squads (*Einsatzgruppen*) 11–12, 18, 24, 26, 29
Monowitz 33
Moskowitz, Daniel 97
Münch, Hans 90
My Life My Way (Wrobel) 103

Nansen, Odd 141
National Socialist German Workers' Party (NSDAP) Program 52
National Socialist program 52–54
nationalism 18
Nazi Party 23, 26
Neustadt 140
Nostra Aetate 147
Nuremberg Laws on Citizenship and Race 10, 39, 44, 54
Nuremberg Trials 20–21, 25, 33, 126–129
Nyholm, Ove 29

Oberheuser, Herta 40–41
Ogilvie-Forbes, George 80
On the Jewish Question (Marx) 50–51
Operation Barbarossa 18, 129
Operation Dragoon 119
Operation Overlord 118
"Operation Reinhard" death camps 5
Oranienburg 9
"Order Police" 34–35
Ordinary Men (Browning) 34–35

Palestine 20, 125
Papenburg 9
Paragraph 175 62
partisans 98, 99–101
Patton, George S. 119
Paul VI, Pope 147
Pechersky, Alexander 115

People's Court (*Volksgerichtshof*) 42–45
Peoples' Receivers 28
Perl, Gisella 138
Perlasca, Giorgio 70
Philadelphia Holocaust Memorial Plaza 149
Pilecki, Witold 113
Pilyar, Yuri 135
Pius XII, Pope 94
Plagge, Karl 90–91
political crimes 42–43
political imprisonment 9
Polonski, Abraham 106, 107
Polonski, Eugénie 106, 107
Porrajamos (The Devouring) 61
prisoner rebellions 97, 101, 113–115
propaganda 27–29
Purgly, Magdolna 74

quisling 46
Quisling, Vidkun 46

Rabinowitz, Dorothy 137, 140
racial antisemitism 17, 18, 20, 28
racial struggle (*Rassenkampf*) 54–55
racially motivated experiments 40
Racine, Mila 67
racism 17
Rassenhygiene see eugenics
Ravensbrück 15, 37, 38, 132, 137
Red Army 118–119
Refugee Children Movement 82–84
Reichstag fire 8–9
religious antisemitism 16, 18
religious belief 139–141
rescuers: British 80–84; overview of 66–68; perpetrators as 89–92; profiles of 70–76; Righteous among the Nations 68–70; upstanders 88–89
Reserve Police Battalion 101 25, 34–35, 101
revenge 138–139
Riegner, Gerhard 86–87
Riegner Telegram 86–87

Righteous among the Nations 67, 68–70, 75, 76
Rise and Fall of the Third Reich, The (Shirer) 67
Robota, Roza 114
Rochczyn, Isaac 97
Röhm, Ernst 62
Roitman, Paul 107
Roma 60–62
Roman Catholic Church 94, 147
Roosevelt, Franklin Delano 77, 94
Rosenberg, Alfred 25
Rousset, David 141–142

Sachsenhausen 31, 72
Safirsztajn, Regina 114
Salkaházi, Sára 74
Salvesen, Sylvia 132
Schindler, Oskar 66, 70
Schindler's List 156
Schmid, Anton 91
Second Generation 156–157
Secret Polish Army (*Tajna Armia Polska*) 113
Semprun, Jorge 142–143
Sh'erit ha-Pletah ("The Saving Remnant") 125
Shirer, William L. and Tess 67
Shoah (calamity, destruction) 8
Shoes on the Danube Promenade memorial 149
Silverman, Samuel 86
Sinti 60–62
sippenhaft 90
Sisters of Social Service 73–74
Slachta, Margit 73–75
Slavic peoples 64–65
Smallbones, Robert 80–81
"Smallbones System" 81
Smolar, Hersh 97
Sobibór 5, 6, 12, 14, 57, 97, 101, 114, 115, 119
Social Darwinism 17, 18, 54
Sondergerichte (Special Courts) 42, 44
Sonderkommando 114

Sonnenstein 55
Spiegel, Edith 56
Spiegel, Fred 56–59
Spielberg, Steven 156
SS (*Schutzstaffel*) 3–4, 5, 24–25, 26, 29
St. Clair Gainer, Donald 81–82
sterilization, forced 55, 61
Stoecker, Adolf 51
Streicher, Julius 27
Strobos, Tina 66
Stroop, Jürgen 112
Stuckart, Wilhelm 44
Sugihara, Chuine "Sempo" 70
survival urge 134–136
Süskind, Walter 67
Szmaglewska, Seweryna 135, 137–138

tales 1–2
Taylor, Myron 78
Tec, Nechama 69
Tenenbaum, Mordechaj 97
Theresienstadt 15, 140
Tillion, Germaine 137
totalitarianism 18
Totenkopf (Death's Head) insignia 24
transit camps 57–58
transmitted trauma 157
Treblinka: Gerstein at 91; ghetto deportations to 102; Hungarian campaign and 14; liberation of 119; prisoner rebellions at 97, 101, 114–115; Roma and 61; unprecedented nature of 5, 6, 12
Trocmé, André 66, 70
Truman, Harry S. 124
Turnour, Edward (Lord Winterton) 78
25 Points 52–54

Union of Military Organization 113–114
United Nations 4, 21, 126, 129–130

United Nations Relief and Rehabilitation Administration 125
United States Holocaust Memorial Museum 150
United Zionist Youth Movement (*Mouvement de la jeunesse sioniste*; MJS) 108–109
Universal Declaration on Human Rights 21
Unsdorfer, S.B. 131–132, 136
upstanders 88–89

Vaivara 119–120
Vernichtungslager (death camp) *see* death camps
Versailles Peace Conference 17, 52
Vichy French officials 24
Vichy regime 45–46
victims, number of 8, 19, 49, 60
Voice of the Spirit 73
Volk, mythical understanding of 17, 26
Volkenrath, Elisabeth 38
vom Rath, Ernst 10–11
Vught 56, 72

Waffen-SS 32, 46
Wajcblum, Estusia 114
Wallenberg, Raoul 66, 70
Wannsee Conference 12, 25, 45
War Crimes 127, 128
War Refugee Board 94
Warsaw Ghetto Uprising 97, 111–112
Wehrmacht 30
Weimar Constitution 9
Wels 126
Welstch, Robert 96
Westerbork 15, 56–59
White Rose 97
Wiesel, Elie 1, 140
Wijsmuller-Meijer, Geertruida 83–84
Wilde-KZ (wild concentration camps) 9
Wilhelm II, Kaiser 51

Winton, Nicholas 84
Wirths, Eduard 41
Wise, Stephen S. 86–87
women as perpetrators 36–39
Worl, Ludwig 114
World War II, outbreak of 11
Wrobel, Eta 98, 101–103

Yad Vashem 67, 69, 70, 72, 75, 76, 150
Yom Hashoah 146

Zionist Organization of France 107
Zuckerman, Yitzhak 112
Żydowski Związek Wojskowy (Jewish Military Union; ŻZW) 112
Zyklon B 14, 32

For Product Safety Concerns and Information please contact our EU
representative GPSR@taylorandfrancis.com
Taylor & Francis Verlag GmbH, Kaufingerstraße 24, 80331 München, Germany

www.ingramcontent.com/pod-product-compliance
Lightning Source LLC
Chambersburg PA
CBHW051740230426
43670CB00012B/2095